BS/FR – GOD'S WAY MADE EASY
Colossians – Friederichsen,
#079   Kay, 1970
Moody Press

BS/FR – GOD'S WAY MADE EASY
Colossians – Friederichsen,
#079   Kay, 1970
Moody Press

GOD'S WAY MADE EASY

Written and Illustrated

by

KAY FRIEDERICHSEN

MOODY PRESS

CHICAGO

ISBN: 0-8024-3039-2

7 8 9 10 11 12 Printing/LC/Year 89 88 87 86 85 84

Printed in the United States of America

CONTENTS

FOREWORD

May the Lord rejoice your heart as you consider the living book of Colossians and experience that God's way is truly easy. This book was written as these lessons were given, so that you might share in the blessing that God's Word has been to my own heart.

The material presented here is limited due to lack of space, but the desire is that some devotional application will encourage you to deeper study of Colossians so that the truth of salvation and victorious life will be more appreciated.

KAY FRIEDERICHSEN

1

POSITION IN CHRIST
Saints and Saintliness (Col 1:1-8)

WHILE A LONELY PRISONER in Rome, the apostle Paul received a visitor, a fellow prisoner by the name of Epaphras who was the founder and minister of the church at Colosse, a town in the province of Asia far north and west of Palestine. The Christians there had heard the message of Paul, although he had never himself visited there. Epaphras came to the apostle in great trouble. He was concerned for the wave of error that seemed to be sweeping the church and even threatened to lead some believers astray from the truth. This error was a combination of heathenism, Judaism and Christianity which had a show of wisdom and human intellectualism, yet propagated philosophies that bordered on paganism.

The letter to the Colossian Christians, then, was God's inspired answer for those days. But it has also met the problems, doubts and errors of every period of church history since then.

The grace of God is seen in action to save the sinner, set apart the saints, and send them forth to serve, as well as to supply them with what they need to meet errors.

9

Since the words are addressed to the "saints in Christ," they are as up to date as tomorrow's newspapers. God's way is easy for those who love Him!

Salutation

COLOSSIANS 1:1—"Paul, an apostle of Jesus Christ by the will of God, and Timotheus our brother."

Paul was qualified as one of the unique apostles, chosen and called by Christ personally, and an eye witness of His resurrected majesty (Ac 9). He wrought the signs of an apostle (2 Co 12:12) as well as being inspired to write most of the books of the New Testament. God has not authorized any apostolic succession since Paul was called, so there are no new apostles living on earth today. Timotheus (Timothy) was not an apostle, but one of Paul's converts and a fellow missionary with Paul.

If there are no apostles today, is there then no representative of God for our times? Indeed, yes! God has not

CHRIST in SAINTS

SAINTS IN CHRIST

left Himself without a witness. The word *apostle* means "a sent one, a missionary," and certainly this calling has not ceased just because the initial apostles are now in glory. The New Testament says clearly that every believer has been sent to give out the gospel which has now been given us. True, there is no new inspiration or revelation now, but all who have received Jesus Christ as personal Saviour are commissioned as messengers and missionaries for God. "Ye shall receive power, after that the Holy Ghost is come upon you: and ye shall be witnesses" (Ac 1:8).

Saints in Christ

COLOSSIANS 1:2—"To the saints and faithful brethren in Christ which are at Colosse."

In Christ is the theme of the prison epistles and this letter to the Colossians. But this is not limited to those in that town alone any more than any scripture is limited to the believers in the churches to which they were addressed. For example, "And when this epistle is read among you, cause that it be read also in the church of the Laodiceans; and that ye likewise read the epistle from Laodicea" (Col 4:16; see also Col 2:1).

Saints *in Christ* are those who have received Him and those whom He has received. This is the description of all believers. God does not choose us *because* we are saintly, but to *make* us saintly! ". . . them that are sanctified in Christ Jesus, called to be saints, with all that in every place call upon the name of Jesus Christ our Lord, both their's and our's" (1 Co 1:2). The saints, then, are those whom God has called and who have called upon

Him. "Whosoever shall call upon the name of the Lord shall be saved" (Ro 10:13). The "called ones" are the "come ones"!

Notice, too, that the saints are on earth. All saints go to heaven when they die, but they do not become saints after they die. Those who are not saints here on earth never go to heaven at all. No church or council can pronounce anyone a saint, for saints *in Christ* are separated and saved by God, to God, in God and through God! It is all His doing by grace. This is our position in Christ. Saints!

Notice again, saints are not perfect while here on earth. This epistle to the Colossians was written to warn the saints against error and sin, and to stir them to saintliness, for sainthood is a possession and a profession and a practice. A saint on earth is not perfect, but he is willing to be!

Did you ever point to a pile of lumber on your empty lot and say, "That's our new home"? It was not yet a house, but you had plans for it!

I remember watching my father as he built our home in Wheaton after he returned from missionary service in China and was teaching at the Moody Bible Institute. We called the confusion of bricks and lumber "the house."

God is in the process of building us into perfect saints, and He knows what He is making of us, although we are definitely yet "in the making" and far from perfect. Perfection will come in glory. "To the end he may stablish your hearts unblameable in holiness before God, even our Father, at the coming of our Lord Jesus Christ" (1 Th 3:13).

Sainthood is eternal. There are ex-presidents and ex-mayors, but there are no ex-saints!

"Brethren in Christ" is another name for saints who are also the children of God. "For ye are all the children of God by faith in Christ Jesus" (Gal 3:26). *In Christ!* This is the *position* of all who have received Jesus Christ as Saviour, and this makes us acceptable with God (Eph 1:6-7).

"Faithful brethren in Christ" refers to "those who have faith in Christ." No one can be faithful until he has faith. "But without faith it is impossible to please him" (Heb 11:6). Saving faith always sanctifies, and the sanctified ones (saints) want to be saintly and faithful. This is the difference between those who *profess* to know Christ and those who *possess* His salvation.

COLOSSIANS 1:2—"Grace be unto you, and peace, from God our Father and the Lord Jesus Christ."

Grace is God's love for the unlovely. By His grace He has provided redemption by the sacrifice of Himself, and by His grace He has called guilty sinners and made them into His saints. Such grace as this can only be appreciated when we take a good look into the mirror of God's holiness and realize how absolutely unworthy any human being (including ourselves) is to be chosen of God.

Grace not only saves but is God's gift to make the saints gracious, saintly and faithful. This is grace for living.

There is grace for suffering too, for God has promised, "My grace is sufficient for thee: for my strength is made perfect in weakness" (2 Co 12:9). Since He "careth for you," why not let Him take the care?

There is also grace for dying. Although a Christian will be with the Lord when he dies, the devil often tries to confuse the believer on the deathbed by saying, "You're not really saved! Think of all your sins!"

One saint who was distressed with doubts as she lay dying found comfort from the promise "For God hath not appointed us to wrath, but to obtain salvation by our Lord Jesus Christ. Who died for us, that whether we wake or sleep, we should live together with him" (1 Th 5:9-10). Praise God, He giveth more grace! This makes God's way easy.

Then, there is grace for those who *go* with the gospel. "As every man hath received the gift, even so minister the same one to another, as good stewards of the manifold grace of God" (1 Pe 4:10). God's grace is "many fold," fold upon fold, endless folds of grace—manifold!

With grace comes peace. Peace *with God* is salvation, but the peace *of God* is experience. Peace is cessation of

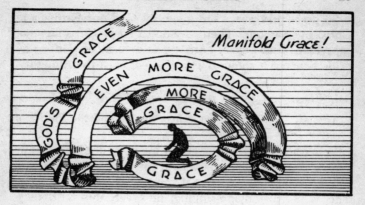

hostilities against God, freedom from fear of damnation, liberation from guilt. "Therefore being justified by faith, we have peace with God through our Lord Jesus Christ: by whom we have access by faith into this grace wherein we stand" (Ro 5:1-2).

The peace of God means rest and trust in important matters, regardless of circumstances. As a babe nestles in her mother's arms without constantly worrying, "Are you holding me tight? You won't drop me, will you?" so we trust in the providence of the almighty arm of God.

Notice, though, that this grace and peace is from God *our Father.* How reassuring it is to know He cares more for us than we care for ourselves. Think of that! But, remember that this gift is only for those who are saints *in Christ,* the born-again sons of God.

Also note that the names of the Father and Jesus Christ are linked together. Why? Because Christ is God. Never could any created being be thus coupled with God.

So grace and peace are given by God our Father and Christ our Saviour. Then why do so many Christians not experience real peace? Anxiety is a form of doubt and pride because it shows that we do not trust the Almighty.

Saintliness

COLOSSIANS 1:3a—"We give thanks to God and the Father of our Lord Jesus Christ."

Being a saint *in Christ* and a member of God's family brings responsibility as well as privilege. Thanks and praise must follow as part of saintliness and faithfulness. This is not just hymn-singing, however; this is "thanks-living," which is saintliness.

COLOSSIANS 1:3b—"Praying always for you."

Unselfishness in prayer makes us more worthy of God's blessing and peace. So many of our prayers are just "Give me, help me, bless me!" Are we on our knees only for *self*, or for souls? (See Eph 6:18.) The more time we spend in prayer and praise, the more the peace that will follow. This is spiritual health.

Someone said to me, "But I don't have any joy in Bible reading and prayer. I don't see answers. I quit!"

I reminded that Christian that we don't quit washing our face just because we don't feel joy in doing it! We need it just the same! When we do not feel like praying, that's the time to pray! We need it just the same. "Praying always."

COLOSSIANS 1:4a—"Since we heard of your faith in Christ Jesus."

This is now the actual step of salvation. Faith *in Christ* is not faith in ourselves or in some church or some religious deeds. Saving faith is not blind "wishing it so," or trying to make it so, or how much faith we have. Rather, saving faith depends upon the One in whom we have faith—Jesus Christ Himself. Saving faith is believing God's Word (Ro 10:17) and receiving God's Son (Jn 1:12), and this results in our living "thank you." Faith is trust in Christ who is the source as well as the object of our faith. "But God, who is rich in mercy, for his great love wherewith he loved us, even when we were dead in sins, hath quickened us together *with Christ*, (by grace ye are saved:) and hath raised us up together, and made us sit together in heavenly places *in Christ Jesus*: that in the ages to come he might shew the exceeding riches of his grace in his kindness toward us *through Christ Jesus*. For by grace are ye saved through faith; and that not of yourselves: it is the gift of God: not of works, lest any man should boast" (Eph 2:4-9).

Then why do some try to earn acceptance with God by joining a church or other similar deeds? Good deeds are only for those who are *in Christ*. It is an insult to offer to pay for a gift which God planned, purchased, procured and proffers free. He also prepares us for the gift of faith, and preserves those who accept it. What grace!

Another thing—saving faith does not depend upon just believing hard enough, or the measure of sincerity. It is possible to believe very hard and be very sincere, and yet be sincerely wrong. There must be connection with God by faith in Christ.

Once when traveling to Dallas to visit my son, I left

my place in the coach to go to the sandwich car. As I passed down the aisles, I met a missionary friend and stopped to chat in her coach. The train kept stopping and starting and shunting back and forth, and eventually I decided to return to my own car. I opened the connecting door and gasped in surprise—the rear section of the train was missing! In panic I asked the brakeman, "Where's the rest of the train?" We were stopped at the moment.

"Where are you going, lady?"

"I'm going to Dallas!"

"Well, we're going to Houston. The Dallas section separated from us a mile back!"

Just then the train started moving, so I hopped off. I didn't want to go to Houston! I'll never forget standing there in the broiling Texas sun watching that train pull away. I didn't even have any shoes on—just slippers!

Then a switch engine came backing down the track.

THE TRAIN PULLED AWAY!

I stood right in its way and waved frantically. They stopped in amazement. But when they understood my plight, they called, "Climb aboard!" I clung for dear life to the rear step as we chugged down the track with the whistle blowing! I caught up with the Dallas train just in time!

Now, I was sincere enough. I thought the entire train was going to Dallas. But I was sincerely wrong! I was not on the train that was "in connection."

COLOSSIANS 1:4b—"And of the love which ye have to all the saints."

Saintliness shows itself by love for all believers, and not just for personal friends. Love is genuine concern, care, courtesy and consideration for others. Love is the delight in and desire for the well-being of the ones loved. This love is to be for all the saints. Sometimes lack of fellowship with God makes Christians uncomfortable among godly people. If they do not love the saints of God, they could not love the Lord very much either.

Security

COLOSSIANS 1:5a—"For the hope which is laid up for you in heaven."

This is now the third of the spiritual threesome: faith, hope and love. Hope looks forward to that which we delight in, long for and know will be waiting for us. This is no "hope so" hope, but rather, "Which hope we have as an anchor of the soul, both sure and stedfast, and which entereth into that within the veil [heaven]; whither the forerunner is for us entered, even Jesus" (Heb 6:19-

HEAVEN

HE hooks us in!

20). The believer is anchored into the rock, Christ Jesus.

This is the "I know it is real, and can't wait for it" hope, even as the starry-eyed bride looks forward to her wedding day, knowing that it will bring her beloved to her side. The world says, "While there's life, there's hope." But the saint *in Christ* has hope even after death— a living hope in a living Lord.

The hope *in Christ* makes us holy. "For the grace of God that bringeth salvation hath appeared to all men, teaching us that, denying ungodliness and worldly lusts, we should live soberly, righteously, and godly, in this present world; looking for the blessed hope, and the glorious appearing of the great God and our Saviour Jesus Christ" (Titus 2:11-13).

Hope *in Christ* makes us happy. "Blessed be the God and Father of our Lord Jesus Christ, which according to his abundant mercy hath begotten us again [we are born again] unto a lively [living] hope by the resurrection of

Jesus Christ from the dead, to an inheritance incorruptible, and undefiled, and that fadeth not away, reserved in heaven for you, who are kept by the power of God" (1 Pe 1:3-5). This should give us wings of praise!

Hope *in Christ* makes us helpful. "Your work of faith, and labour of love, and patience of hope in our Lord Jesus Christ" (1 Th 1:3). This hope of glory is not based upon the fact that we are faithful, but on the fact that He is faithful.

PRAISE!

"Now the God of hope fill you with all joy and peace in believing, that ye may abound in hope, through the power of the Holy Ghost" (Ro 15:13). This is a "know so" hope!

COLOSSIANS 1:5*b*—"Whereof ye heard before in the word of the truth of the gospel."

Just how does this message of hope come to us? Through the word of the truth of the gospel. "For our gospel came not unto you in word only, but also in power, and in the Holy Ghost, and in much assurance" (1 Th 1:5a).

The "word" is the person of God revealed in Christ, and expressed in the Bible, the written Word. The living Word is God Himself (Jn 1:1-3, 14; Rev 19:13), and this is Jesus Christ. The inspired Scriptures are the expression of God.

The "truth" is the character and mind of God expressed in Jesus Christ, who said, "I am the way, the truth, and the life: no man cometh unto the Father, but by me" (Jn 14:6). There can be no mistake or untruth in the Bible any more than in God Himself.

The "gospel" is the good news of God's Son, the love and provision of God expressed in Jesus Christ for man's salvation. "I am not ashamed of the gospel of Christ: for it is the power of God unto salvation to every one that believeth" (Ro 1:16). Remember, good news certainly is not a message that we must earn our salvation and endure unto the end. That is hopeless news!

Service

COLOSSIANS 1:6a—"Which is come unto you, as it is in all the world."

All the world in Paul's time was the known civilized area where the persecuted Christians had been scattered like seed in the fields and had taken the gospel with them. Their message is also our message: the word of the truth of the gospel! It is as relevant for us as for them. There is no need to rewrite the Bible or update it or apologize for it; it just needs to be reread. Since human behavior has not changed for the good, and God has not changed, and the way of salvation has not changed, then why do men formulate committees and councils to try to modernize religion?

Someone has told us the word of the truth of the gospel, and now someone else is waiting for us to tell it to them. God first calls us to "come and believe!" Then He says, "Go and tell!"

COLOSSIANS 1:6b—"And bringeth forth fruit, as it doth also in you, since the day ye heard it."

The gospel does not wear out with age, wear thin from use or become threadbare from the many who have received it. This living message brings forth living fruit. This reminds me of the banana tree which only exists for the purpose of bearing one bunch of bananas. If it is cut down before the bananas are formed, new shoots keep springing up until it bears those bananas! No wonder many in Colosse heard the gospel from the Christians who began witnessing as soon as they were saved!

Fruit-bearing, however, is not just witnessing or a public ministry. This fruit of the Spirit must begin by bearing fruit in us personally. "The fruit of the Spirit is love, joy, peace, longsuffering, gentleness, goodness, faith [faithfulness], meekness, temperance" (Gal 5:22-23). God wants to work *in us* before He can work *through us*, and thus we "shall neither be barren nor unfruitful in the knowledge of our Lord Jesus Christ" (2 Pe 1:8).

COLOSSIANS 1:6c—"And knew the grace of God in truth."

The saints at Colosse really knew the Lord and His Word, and they had experienced God's grace in salvation and service. This is the secret for our labors in the Lord too. When we apply ourselves wholly to the Lord and the Word, and then apply the Word wholly to ourselves, we can see fruit.

While crossing the Pacific on our way to the mission field, we met a godless fellow with a loud mouth and a rough manner. My husband made it a practice to use an apt scripture whenever suitable in the conversation, until one day that man exploded by saying, "Why don't you think for yourself? Why do you always quote that Bible of yours?"

Paul smiled. "I'd rather think God's thoughts after Him," he said. "I really don't have any better ideas of my own!" The man grunted, but he had no answer.

COLOSSIANS 1:7—"As ye also learned of Epaphras our dear fellowservant, who is for you a faithful minister."

This speaks well of the minister who had won those Colossians, and one might be tempted to say, "Good for him!" But we were not given the Scriptures just so that we might admire the servants of God who lived almost two thousand years ago. This is the example for every saint *in Christ*. The word "fellowservant" means "witness, minister, soul-winner."

Can this be said about us? What kind of ministers are we? Are we preaching by our life and lips and faithful attendance in a Bible-believing, Bible-preaching and Bible-practicing church? Can God say about us that we are faithful ministers in our home or business or school? If we are saints, then we are saved to be saintly, to be sent and to be serving.

COLOSSIANS 1:8—"Who also declared unto us your love in the Spirit."

We have seen that the saints are *"in Christ"* and *"in the Father,"* but now they are said to be *"in the Spirit."* The triune God is involved in our sainthood. Imagine! How then can we be satisfied to limp along at half-mast as Christians when the almighty Trinity has given us faith, hope and love? The believer is to be a producer and not just a consumer—to give out what has been taken in. Why wait for others to show love to us? Begin by showing love to them!

"I thank my God always on your behalf, for the grace of God which is given you by Jesus Christ; that in every thing ye are enriched by him, in all utterance, and in all knowledge; even as the testimony of Christ was confirmed in you: so that ye come behind in no gift; waiting for the coming of our Lord Jesus Christ: who shall confirm you unto the end, that ye may be blameless in the day of our Lord Jesus Christ. God is faithful, by whom ye were called unto the fellowship of his Son Jesus Christ our Lord" (1 Co 1:4-9).

God's way is easy!

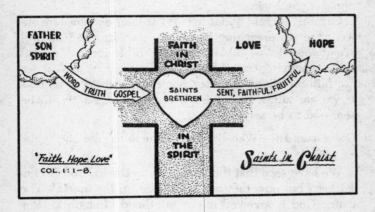

QUESTIONS

1. Why was Epaphras in Rome? (Phile 23)
2. Do others take the place of the twelve in "apostolic succession"? (Rev 21:14)
3. Are all saints perfect? (1 Co 3:1-3; Heb 5:11-14)
4. Who should be faithful? (Eph 1:1; Rev 17:14)
5. Are all men the spiritual children of God? (Jn 8:44; Eph 2:2-3; Ro 9:8; Jn 3:3; Gal 3:26; 1 Jn 3:9)
6. How do good works fit in with saving faith? (Eph 2:10)
7. Who is the "Rock"? (1 Co 10:4; 1 Pe 2:4-8)

8. Who first preached the gospel? (Heb 2:3-4)
9. Can salvation be earned? (2 Ti 1:9, 12; Titus 3:5)
10. Is the Bible now out of date? (Is 46:10; 1 Co 4:17; 1 Th 5:27; 1 Pe 1:25)

2

POSITIVE CHRISTIANS

Victorious Living (Col 1:9-14)

FROM THE VERY HEART of God comes this prayer which was inspired through the apostle Paul for spiritual victory for all saints. Notice how the emphasis is for spiritual blessing rather than mere material or physical things which are too often deemed so very important.

COLOSSIANS 1:9a—"For this cause we also, since the day we heard it, do not cease to pray for you."

From the time Paul heard of the saints *in Christ* in Colosse and their faith, hope and love, he was concerned for their continued growth and maturity *in Christ*, that they might be positive, strong and victorious, a glorious temple unto the Lord.

Imagine a glistening white marble temple that shines in the sunlight almost as if it were lighted from within. The foundation of solid stones supports graceful pillars that lead to the pinnacle at the top. Let this represent the temple of God, the person and character of the positive Christian in which the Spirit of God has complete control.

The Filling of the Positive Christian

COLOSSIANS 1:9b—"That ye might be filled with the knowledge of his will in all wisdom and spiritual understanding."

This is the crowning glory of the Christian life: to be filled with the knowledge of the will of God! But what does this mean in practical everyday language?

To begin with, wisdom and spiritual understanding begin when we receive the Author of wisdom, Jesus Christ, as our Saviour. "In whom are hid all the treasures of wisdom and knowledge" (Col 2:3).

Next, to be filled with the knowledge of His will involves our personal willingness to read, hear, meditate upon, apply and remember, as well as obey, what He has said in His Word. Then, and only then, are we ready to use the wisdom He gives therein, for we can only use what we have absorbed and made our own. God gives no new message, no new truth "from the blue," but He speaks to the mind that is in tune with His Word, and that is filled with the Spirit.

This is not just "What shall I do in this or that instance?" but rather, "What place does the Lord have in my life?" Are we filled (taken over, controlled) by His will? This leaves no place for the devil or *self*. This is spiritual health and victory!

But just how does this come about? Certainly not by striving and agonizing, but by allowing Him to take His rightful place as Director of our thoughts, desires, ambitions, words and deeds. The saints become indwelt by the Spirit of Christ, the Holy Spirit, at the moment of salvation. "If any man have not the Spirit of Christ, he is none of his" (Ro 8:9*b*).

The filling of the Spirit is the moment-by-moment yielding to Him in everything, and this makes God's way easy.

> The dearest idol I have known, whate'er that idol
> be;
> Help me to tear it from Thy throne, and worship
> only Thee!

God commands, "Be not drunk with wine, wherein is excess; but be filled with the Spirit" (Eph 5:18). This is a command, so it is not speaking of a mountain-peak experience but of the normal pattern of living for a saint *in Christ*. The meaning is "be ye constantly being filled." We are indwelt by the Spirit at salvation and this happens once—for all time—but we are to be constantly filled day by day and moment by moment as we yield to Him.

What is meant by not being drunk with wine in contrast to being filled with the Spirit? What is the connection? Those who are drunk with wine are completely taken over by alcohol and are under its control. People of this godless world seek many external things to bolster their ego when they are depressed or fearful, so they turn to liquor, tobacco, narcotics and "happenings"—anything or everything that might fill the empty void within their heart. Saints *in Christ*, however, are commandéd to let the Spirit of God fill them with wisdom and spiritual understanding; therefore, they need no external aid to peace and joy. This is the normal Christian life for the positive and saintly saint. Not to be filled with the Spirit and will of God is to be a spiritual freak.

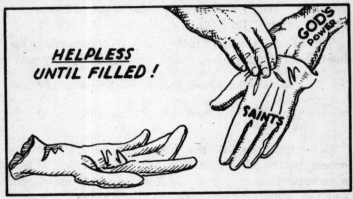

Suppose I said to the gloves that I use when drawing on the blackboard with colored chalk, "Here, gloves, here is the chalk. Now, begin to draw!" Nothing would happen! I might coax them along by saying, "Now, come on, gloves, you have five fingers and you have drawn for me many times, so get busy!" But they do not move! It is only when I slip my hand into them and fill them that they can respond and pick up the chalk and draw! So, as empty gloves we lie helpless until the Spirit of God takes us over and controls us.

Whatever fills the mind will be spoken by the mouth and practiced in the life. Christians often talk fluently about television personalities and world affairs and the neighbors' quarrels and their last operation. But when it comes to the things of the Lord, they are conversation dropouts!

A new convert was so thrilled with the Word of God that she persuaded her husband and daughter to attend a Bible class with her. On the way home afterward, her husband remarked, "I'll have to admit it was tremendous, but I'll never get involved."

He kept coming though, and I finally asked him, "Does this make sense to you? Do you believe that you need the Saviour, and that Christ is the Saviour?"

His answer was short and to the point. "No, I really don't!"

I left him alone as he came week after week, and then again asked him, "How about it now? Do you need the Saviour?"

This time he said soberly, "Yes, I do."

With his wife and daughter we prayed together as he asked Christ to take over his life. Then I turned to the girl and asked, "Have you ever received Christ as your Saviour?"

"Yes," she said, "I did so here two weeks ago after the class." It was a joyful night as that family was united in Christ.

They brought the grandmother to the classes, and she, too, accepted the Lord. Not too long afterward she died, and how her familly thanked God that they had brought her to hear the Word! That family has brought others. Just to see their radiant faces is a tonic!

"Filled with the knowledge of his will!" The pinnacle!

The Faithfulness of the Positive Christian

COLOSSIANS 1:10a—"That ye might walk worthy of the Lord unto all pleasing."

The result of the Christian being filled by the Holy Spirit and controlled by Him is to walk worthy of the Lord! How can we ever do this? *We can't!* This is the work of God in the positive Christian, so there is no excuse for defeated, weak Christians who are still wallowing in self-pity and failure, which is *Self*.

To "walk" speaks of continuing on day by day in normal and healthy Christian living, and not just during revival week! "As ye have received of us how ye ought to walk and to please God, so ye would abound more and more" (1 Th 4:1). What a privilege!

What does "unto all pleasing" mean? How can we please everyone? We can't, and we don't try! This means that we are to be pleasing *to God* in all things. In the case of a troublesome church member who accused the pastor of not pleasing all his parishioners, he quietly replied, "I'm not trying to please them all. I'm only interested in pleasing one Person—the Lord!"

"In all things pleasing" means "through and through"— at home or in public, at school or in business, in social circles or in church. How do we measure up?

During a stage performance, the lights are aglitter and shining. But if you go backstage, what do you see? Ropes, ladders, rough boards and sweating stagehands! But the Christian's life is to be pleasing to the Lord through and through. God's will is that "the man of God may be perfect [complete], throughly furnished unto all good works" (2 Ti 3:17).

COLOSSIANS 1:10b—"Being fruitful in every good work, and increasing in the knowledge of God."

Good works are God-directed deeds as commanded for believers in the New Testament, and they are also God-glorifying deeds. The unsaved man can do nothing good in the sight of God. "Every good work" includes every branch of Christian experience; there is no selective service here! The fruitful life is an obedient life to God's known will that we be saintly, that we study His Word, that we pray without ceasing, that we gather together

fruitful in each branch

for worship and preaching, that we be a testimony to others, that we give of our time, talents and tithes as offerings for His service, and that we be filled with the Spirit.

No saved person should say, "I'll sing in the choir, but I won't give any offering!" or, "I'll lead a moral life, but I won't be baptized!" or, "I'll read my Bible, but I won't go to church!" That is deliberate disobedience to God, and that is sin. "For rebellion is as the sin of witchcraft, and stubbornness is as iniquity and idolatry. Because thou hast rejected the word of the LORD . . ." (1 Sa 15:23).

On the other hand, it is possible for a Christian to teach Sunday school or even pastor a church, and yet his deeds not to be accounted good in God's eyes. If they are done for self-glory or self-gain or self-gratification, then they are not "good works" to the glory of God. "Being filled with the fruits of righteousness, which are by Jesus Christ, unto the glory and praise of God" (Phil 1:11). Every good work is God's work in us and through us as we increase in the knowledge of Him, and this depends upon the measure that we are saturated with His Word. Listen to this verse: "Hear, O Israel, the statutes and judgments which I speak in your ears this day, that ye may *learn* them, and *keep*, and *do* them" (Deu 5:1). This is God's way made easy!

There is no new teaching, no new doctrine, no new Scripture. But what God has given should be our bread and meat and honey and milk, and we will need it as long as we live. Some say, "I don't need to attend Bible classes. I've had Bible courses!" But no one ever says, "I don't need to eat Sunday dinner, since I ate last week!"

Why, they're the first to tie on their bib at dinnertime!

How important that we increase in the knowledge of God! Not just in information about Him, but in contact and fellowship with Him!

COLOSSIANS 1:11a—"Strengthened with all might, according to his glorious power."

This glorious power is the might of the Almighty which is greater than the devil and greater than our need for our impossible situation, or job, or homelife, or unexplainable teenager! When God is allowed to take over a life, He gives power in proportion to His glorious power, and that really is *power!* "As thy days, so shall thy strength be. . . . The eternal God is thy refuge, and underneath are the everlasting arms" (Deu 33:25b-27). When the saint is indwelt by the Spirit of God, he is also to know "what is the exceeding greatness of his power to us-ward who believe, according to the working of his mighty power, which he wrought in Christ, when he raised him from the dead" (Eph 1:19-20).

COLOSSIANS 1:11b—"Unto all patience and longsuffering with joyfulness."

Just what is the power of God for in the life of the positive Christian? To make a name for ourselves and be a great success in the public eye? No! This is not to squander on self. This is to give us patience and longsuffering with joyfulness. Did you note that? God never tells us to do anything He will not give us power to do. His glorious power is not just to remove trials, but rather to give us patience with joyfulness. His "all might" is

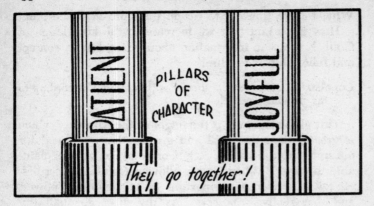

PATIENT

PILLARS OF CHARACTER

JOYFUL

They go together!

sufficient for "all trials" that we may have. This is no martyr spirit of gritting the teeth and bearing it, but active love with joy—even in miseries!

Yes, God wants His children to be happy, but in a way that will help and not hinder them. Joyfulness is a result of victory. Patience, long-suffering and joyfulness, as well as walking worthy of the Lord and being fruitful in every good work, are all part of the structure of the temple of the positive Christian character. They are the pillars that are obvious to the world.

COLOSSIANS 1:12a—"Giving thanks unto the Father."

Here again is the challenge to praise! How could anything less than praise follow the gift of the power of God? So why do we praise so little? A praiseful Christian is a positive Christian, and how the devil hates to hear men praise the Lord! So let's make him miserable! "Let us offer the sacrifice of praise to God continually . . . giving thanks to his name" (Heb 13:15). When we give thanks to God we will be loving and joyful, and then everyone—even the cat and dog—will be able to tell the difference!

"Giving thanks" means that there is to be a continuous action of giving thanks; we are to "keep on giving thanks." This is not just a turkey dinner once a year. After all, if we are going to praise Him throughout all eternity, we had better get in practice now. Thank Him, no matter what!

The Foundation of the Positive Christian

COLOSSIANS 1:12b—"The Father, which hath made us meet to be partakers of the inheritance of the saints in light."

The foundation of the entire temple of positive Christian living is completely the work of God's grace by placing us *in Christ* and *on Christ*. None of us are fit for salvation, but He makes us qualified by His grace to become the children of the King of kings! "Meet" means to be made fit, acceptable, suitable to be partakers. Furthermore, He keeps on making us fit as long as we allow Him.

Who are the saints in light? Some are in heaven with Christ, who is the light of the world, while others are still living on earth. "That ye may be blameless and harmless, the sons of God, without rebuke, in the midst of a crooked and perverse nation, among whom ye shine as lights in the world; holding forth the word of life" (Phil 2:15-16). That which is within us is to shine out. Light is the best police force! So the saints in light include the perfect ones in glory and the willing-to-be-perfect ones here on earth who are right with God. "If we walk in the light, as he is in the light, we have fellowship one with another, and the blood of Jesus Christ his Son cleanseth [continues to cleanse] us from all sin" (1 Jn 1:7).

The inheritance of the saints includes God's presence with us now, His forgiveness of sin, plus future security with Him in glory. "In whom also we have obtained an inheritance, being predestinated according to the purpose of him who worketh all things after the counsel of his own will: that we should be to the praise of his glory, who first trusted in Christ" (Eph 1:11-12).

COLOSSIANS 1:13—"Who hath delivered us from the power of darkness, and hath translated us into the kingdom of his dear Son."

Here is another foundation stone of the positive Christian. God has delivered us, and this is still the work of His grace.

In Scripture "darkness" refers to sin, ignorance and

trouble, and the author of all these is the devil, whose whole intent is to damn the lost and trip up the saved. Satan hates to lose a customer! "For we wrestle not against flesh and blood, but against principalities, against powers, against the rulers of the darkness of this world, against spiritual wickedness" (Eph 6:12).

Satan is not an atheist; he believes every word in the Bible! But he does not accept it or receive the Saviour. He believes and trembles (Ja 2:19), which is more than some foolish men do. There are no atheists in hell. For although atheists go to hell when they die, they do not remain atheists when they get there. They all believe there is a God, but it is too late to be saved.

The saints have been delivered and liberated from the kingdom of darkness. "For ye were sometimes darkness, but now are ye light in the Lord: walk as children of light. And have no fellowship with the unfruitful works of darkness, but rather reprove them" (Eph 5:8, 11).

Just as books are translated from one language to another, so the children of God have been lifted from the kingdom of the devil and are now citizens of another world. Just as an airplane rises above the law of gravity because the power its motors produce is stronger than gravity, so the power of God lifts us above the pull of damnation, death and the kingdom of Satan. "For the law [the principle] of the Spirit of life in Christ Jesus hath made me free from the law of sin and death" (Ro 8:2). "Translated" means "to be caught up, lifted up, changed from a lower to a higher (in the spiritual sense), a change of king and kingdom."

Colossians 1:14—"In whom we have redemption through his blood, even the forgiveness of sins."

This is the final foundation stone of the positive Christian—redemption and forgiveness. But, notice first that this verse begins with those words "In whom." This brings us back to the truth of the saints *in Christ*, placed in Him by the grace of God.

There is no need for forgiveness if there is no sin, no need for redemption if there is no damnation. Sin stems from the root, the heart, the self. The remedy is to hit the root itself, because all lying, stealing, hatred, ill temper and every other sin of the human heart can only be nipped when the heart is dealt with by coming to God. He can neither overlook sin nor erase it without cause, for He has already pronounced the death penalty and He will not go back on His word nor change His mind. He does not say, "Oh, you poor human beings. I'm so sorry for you that I'll just overlook your sin!"

HIT THE ROOT!

Only the payment of the death penalty could satisfy the justice of the divine Judge, and only the paid death penalty could reveal the love of the divine Saviour; and only the death penalty paid by God Himself could be sufficient for all time and all believers and for all sins. "If we confess our sins, he is faithful and just to forgive us our sins, and to cleanse us from all unrighteousness" (1 Jn 1:9).

The repentant sinner is bought back from slavery. Not from human slave markets, but from the slavery of Satan and sin. This applies to those who are wallowing in the gutter on skid row as well as to Mr. and Mrs. Respectable who are slaves to ambition, lust and gold. What a wonderful God "who gave himself for us, that he might redeem us from all iniquity, and purify unto himself a peculiar [special] people, zealous of good works" (Titus 2:14)!

A worm in the center of a circle of burning leaves might struggle to escape until it finds that there is no way out, and then it would lie down to die. Then you could pick it up and set it free. Certainly God has not built a fire around us, but we have built it around ourselves. We have tried to work our own way out and are as helpless as that worm. It is only when we give up and accept God's way of salvation that He can lift us to safety. This is grace! "In whom we have redemption through his blood, the forgiveness of sins, according to the riches of his grace" (Eph 1:7).

God is waiting for contrite hearts to accept His redemption and forgiveness by receiving the Saviour who died to pay our death penalty, and then we will be united with

Him. How sad when men bypass the Saviour and try to make their own way! "For they being ignorant of God's righteousness, and going about to establish their own righteousness, have not submitted themselves unto the righteousness of God" (Ro 10:3). This is like a tiger trying to rub off his stripes in the grass!

The forgiveness of sins is only possible when the sinner comes to accept the Sin-bearer, Christ. This is God's Sin-eradicator! "Ye were not redeemed with corruptible things, as silver and gold. . . . But with the precious blood of Christ" (1 Pe 1:18-19). His blood is precious because it is the blood that God shed on Calvary. "By his own blood . . . having obtained eternal redemption for us" (Heb 9:12).

But exactly when does this redemption take place in our life? "In whom we *have* redemption." Right now! The moment we receive Him, that day becomes salvation day, and we are *in Him*. "Repent ye therefore, and be converted, that your sins may be blotted out" (Ac 3:19).

So now, as God has given us this view of the temple of the positive Christian, just how do we fit into the pattern? Are we on the foundation—on Christ? Are we showing forth the pillars of saintly living by living in victory? Are we filled with the Spirit—the very peak of saintliness?

"Furthermore then we beseech you, brethren, and exhort you by the Lord Jesus, that as ye have received of us how ye ought to walk and to please God, so ye would abound more and more" (1 Th 4:1).

God's way is easy!

QUESTIONS

1. How does man's wisdom compare with God's? (1 Co 1:19-30)
2. What should fill the mind of the saint? (Ps 119:10-11, 97)

3. Who fills the Christian's heart? (Eph 3:16-21)
4. What is the spiritual walk? (Gal 5:16, 25; 1 Th 2:12)
5. Why should the redeemed do good works? (Titus 2:14; Heb 10:24-25)
6. What gives the power of God? (2 Co 6:6-7; 13:4)
7. Why should saints give thanks? (1 Co 15:57; 2 Co 9:15; 2:14)
8. Who are the saints in light on earth? (Ro 13:12-14; Eph 5:8-11)
9. What is God's part in forgiveness? (Ps 32:1-2; 103:12; Heb 8:12; 10:17)
10. What is the believer's part in forgiveness? (Ps 32:5; 1 Jn 1:9)

3

POWERFUL CREATOR
Christ Is God (Col 1:15-19)

"Oh, I believe the Bible, and that Jesus came to be the Saviour, but I don't see why I need to believe He is God. I never heard such a thing before! Isn't it enough to believe in the Saviour?" This was a question asked by a visitor to our classes.

No, it is not enough! Christ could not be the Saviour if He were not God, for the Bible would be a lie, Christ would be the greatest fraud of all history, and there would be no remedy for sin. This is why the doctrine of the deity of Christ is a *must*. It shines forth as a jewel in the dark sky of this sin-soaked world and is the keystone of all Christian faith.

Christ and God

Colossians 1:15a—"Who is the image of the invisible God."

God is invisible because He is spirit. A spirit is a person. God is the eternal Person, the Creator of all others, and is not limited to a physical body or to material things or to finite conditions or to time. He lives in the eternal present.

Then what does the Bible mean when it says Jesus Christ is the image of the invisible God? How can He be the image of One who has no image?

The Bible is speaking of the character and "person image" of God—the identical mirror image of the attributes and identity of the Almighty, for Christ is Himself God.

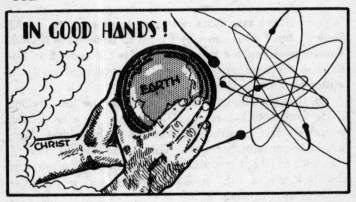

Note this description of Jehovah, the Almighty: "Now unto the King eternal, immortal, invisible, the only wise God, be honour and glory for ever and ever. Amen" (1 Ti 1:17). Then note how these same attributes are ascribed to the Lord Jesus: "Our Lord Jesus Christ: which in his times he shall shew [He will show Himself], who is the blessed and only Potentate, the King of kings, and Lord of lords; who only hath immortality, dwelling in the light which no man can approach unto; whom no man hath seen, nor can see: to whom be honour and power everlasting. Amen" (1 Ti 6:14-16).

This book of Colossians was written to warn against the errors which are as much in evidence today as they were then. Men believed that between themselves and God was a long line of shadowy beings who demanded worship and pacification, and that Jesus was just one of these.

Scripture states that Christ is actually God. "No man hath seen God at any time; the only begotten Son, which is in the bosom of the Father, he hath declared him" (Jn 1:18). Jesus Christ is the "brightness of his [God's] glory, and the express image of his person, and upholding all things by the word of his power, when he had by himself purged our sins, sat down on the right hand of the Majesty on high" [Heb 1:3]. Christ is the actual character and substance and person of God. The invisible God was made visible and comprehensible by Christ who became the God-Man.

It was for this very purpose that He came to earth, and said, "He that hath seen me hath seen the Father" (Jn 14:9). He fills the sin chasm between God and sinners, for He is the "one mediator between God and man, the man Christ Jesus; who gave himself a ransom" (1 Ti 2:5-6). Evidence is not lacking, but men are lacking in willingness to believe. God reveals Himself in three Persons: God the Father, God the Son, and God the Holy Spirit. All three Persons are fully God, yet All are one God.

Transport yourself into eternity past and see the triune God already in existence before the creation of the world. Even at that time God knew what He would create and that human beings would sin and need a remedy. There is no surprise with Him. He also knew what He would do about salvation, for this was no "hurry up and find an answer" matter. He had already planned to give Himself to be the Sin-bearer.

Therefore, the death of Jesus on the cross of Calvary was already an accomplished fact as far as God was concerned, even before He made man. Jesus is called "the Lamb slain from the foundation of the world" (Rev 13:8), and "Christ . . . a lamb without blemish and without spot: who verily was foreordained before the foundation of the world" (1 Pe 1:19-20).

With God the future is *now*. This is why much of prophecy in the Bible was written in the present or even the past tense although it had not yet come to pass. So, in the mind of God, Christ had already been born in the flesh and had died and risen again, even before the creation.

What a comfort to realize that God knows the future as well as the past! We certainly need not worry about tomorrow, for God is already there! Certainly we need not resort to psychic soothsayers to tell us the future, for all that God wants us to know about the future is already written in the Bible. He will give no further information. Jesus told His disciples, "It is not for you to know the times or the seasons, which the Father hath put in his own power" (Ac 1:7). God is not going to give advance information about the stock market or the weather or world events! He especially does not tell the future to those who hold wrong doctrine. "The secret things belong unto the LORD our God: but those things which are revealed belong unto us and to our children for ever, that we may do all the words of this law" (Deu 29:29).

COLOSSIANS 1:15b—"The firstborn of every creature."

What is meant when Jesus is called the "firstborn"? This certainly is not referring to His origin, for He was not created. He is the preexistent and self-existent One. Fathom that if you can!

Christ is the One who caused all creation to be born. "The Amen, the faithful and true witness, the beginning of the creation of God" (Rev 3:14). He is called the "only begotten Son of God" because of His unique position and relationship with God the Father in contrast to human beings who become the sons of God by faith in Him. God is the *eternal Father* (yet none can be called a father until he has a son) and Christ is the *eternal Son*. "When he bringeth in the firstbegotten into the world, he saith, And let all the angels of God worship him. But

ETERNAL SON

The begotten Son
(BEGOTTEN IN THE FLESH)

unto the Son he saith, Thy throne, O God, is for ever and ever" (Heb 1:6, 8). Remember that worship is to be given only to God.

He was begotten in the flesh when He came into the world, but He did not begin to exist then (Is 9:6; Mic 5:2).

Then, too, Jesus is said to have been begotten from the dead at His resurrection. "The firstborn from the dead" (Col 1:18), and, "He hath raised up Jesus again; as it is also written in the second psalm, Thou art my Son, this day have I begotten thee" (Ac 13:33).

Someone argues, "But why include Jesus? Why have another God?"

He is not another God. He *is* God—equal with the Father and the Spirit. It is well to be honest and admit that our finite minds cannot comprehend the doctrine of the Trinity any more than we can fathom eternity or infinity or the sovereignty of God, for His thoughts are higher than our thoughts and His ways higher than our ways.

The triune God is involved in our salvation. "Elect according to the foreknowledge of God the *Father*, through sanctification of the *Spirit*, unto obedience and sprinkling of the blood of *Jesus Christ*" (1 Pe 1:2).

Jesus Christ was the Son of God before the creation of every being or thing. His is now reclaimed glory, not acquired glory.

Christ and Creation

COLOSSIANS 1:16*a*—"For by him were all things created."

The preexistent Christ is the Author and Agent who created everything. This is the answer to another of the errors of the Colossian days as well as now: since man is evil and man is involved with matter, therefore all matter is evil. But this is fallacy, for God created matter and He saw that it was good. Things have no morality as such; they are good or bad only as man uses them rightly or wrongly.

COLOSSIANS 1:16—"For by him were all things created, that are in heaven, and that are in earth, visible and invisible, whether they be thrones, or dominions, or principalities, or powers: all things were created by him, and for him."

Things were created; they did not evolve! "Through faith we understand that the worlds [ages] were framed by the word of God, so that things which are seen were not made of things which do appear" (Heb 11:3). To create is to make out of nothing, and God made His perfect creation out of nothing. He said, "Let there be" and there was. "In the beginning God created the heaven and the earth" (Gen 1:1). Yet, now we find that Jesus Christ created the heaven and the earth! He is God!

Things in heaven would be the created heavens, the atmosphere around our earth as well as the universe beyond (not the heaven of God which was also preexistent before the creation of the earth); invisible things would be the spirit world (created persons). Principalities and powers usually refer to the kingdom of Lucifer (Satan's dynasty, and not mere earthly kingdoms), the kingdom of darkness.

There is always the question as to why the Lord created

Satan (Lucifer) when He knew he would be such a problem. One might just as well ask, "Why did He create me, when He knew I would be such a problem?" When we reach glory, we'll understand! One thing is certain though. There can be no testing without a test, and no decision without a tempter, and no real love without a choice. God does not want puppets on a string, but responsible beings who will choose to love Him, and whom He can love and bless and fellowship with throughout eternity future.

COLOSSIANS 1:17—"And he is before all things, and by him all things consist."

This does not say He *was* before all things, for He lives in the eternal present where there is no past, present or future, and before creation *he is*. By Him all things hold together (consist). The hand that holds the universe together and brought order out of confusion and cosmos out of chaos is the same hand that continues to hold it together and is keeping it all running until the end of the world when He will create new heavens and a new earth. This is the hand that was nailed to the cross of Calvary for our sins. Amazing grace!

Christ keeps the cycles of nature in order, prevents atoms from splitting at the wrong time, creates life and allows death. No, God is not dead! He's not even sick! Doesn't the devil wish He were! It is unbelievable that men would attribute creation to Mother Nature or natural causes for, after all, who made natural causes?

Christ and Resurrection

COLOSSIANS 1:18b—"The firstborn from the dead."

God could not die. Therefore, He took upon Himself the form of man and, as man, He died. It was human blood that was spilled on Calvary, but it was God who gave His blood (Ac 20:28). He did not come only to preach the gospel; He came *to be* the gospel and to pay the price to redeem His church with His own blood. "For ye are bought with a price" (1 Co 6:20).

At such a price, can it be that He is being short-changed when it comes to our response to Him? He paid for our souls, our time and talents, and our talk and thoughts. Are we robbing Him? Is He getting His money's worth? Are we thieves?

For a resurrection there must first be a death. Only death could pay the penalty for sin. "The wages of sin is death" (Ro 6:23). But He did not die and remain dead; neither did He swoon and revive. He died and rose again. "Christ died for our sins according to the

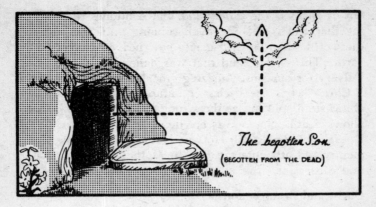

The begotten Son
(BEGOTTEN FROM THE DEAD)

scriptures . . . he rose again the third day according to the scriptures" (1 Co 15:3-4). It is as simple as that. As the Creator of life He was able, of course, to give Himself resurrection life, thus proving His deity. He promised that He would raise Himself from the dead (Jn 10:17-18), and He also promised that the saints would be resurrected to live with Him. "Because I live, ye shall live also" (Jn 14:19*b*). "I am the resurrection and the life: he that believeth in me, though he were dead, yet shall he live" (Jn 11:25; see also 1 Co 6:14).

It is always sad to hear these glorious promises recited over the dead bodies of unbelievers, for there is no promise of hope for those who have rejected the Saviour. To them, Christ says, "Ye shall . . . die in your sins: whither I go, ye cannot come" (Jn 8:21*b*). They will be resurrected, but it will be the resurrection of damnation into the lake of fire with the devil and his angels in everlasting existence of torment.

Christic and the Church

COLOSSIANS 1:18a—"And he is the head of the body, the church."

The "church" is another collective term for all the called saints since the beginning of this church age when the Holy Spirit came to indwell the believers. This called-out assembly is also called the bride of Christ and His body. The church is a people and not a place, a body of believers and not a building. Christ is the Head, the authority, the Coordinator and the Ruler as well as the Bridegroom for His bride. There can be no living body without a head! "The head over all things to the church, which is his body" (Eph 1:22-23). Wonder of wonders, the body lives as long as the head does! This is security! The only way that a saved saint *in Christ* could be lost again would be for Christ to be lost! This is impossible!

Christ the Head

The Church
HIS BODY

Christ and You and Me

COLOSSIANS 1:18c—"That in all things he might have the preeminence."

This is addressed to the church, the saints. Christ is to be the Head. Number one! Worldly philosophy says, "Take care of number one!" and they are referring to *self*. But for a saint *in Christ*, number one should be the Saviour, the Head. Our life is a trust and not a gift. Since He put us first when He died on the cross, we should now allow Him the preeminence that is His due. No one else should ever be called "His Eminence"!

Preeminence means first place. This is the place that Jesus has in heaven and will have through all eternity. "And there shall be no more curse: but the throne of God and of the Lamb shall be in it [God and Christ have one throne]; and his servants shall serve him [the singular pronoun is used for both God and Christ, for They are one]: and they shall see his face [all Scripture tells us that it will be the face of Christ that we shall see in glory]; and his name shall be in their foreheads" (Rev 22:3-4). So Christ is God. May we say with the apostle Paul, "But what things were gain to me, those I counted loss for Christ. . . . I count all things but loss for the excellency of the knowledge of Christ Jesus my Lord" (Phil 3:7-8).

Are you wondering just how this relates to you and me? If you have never received Christ as your Saviour, then you are rejecting almighty God Himself. Is this what you want? Surely not! This is now the time to pray and

ask Him to be your Lord and your God. Then see if God's way is not made easy!

But for us who are Christians, can it be that we are putting ourselves ahead of the Lord? Is our *self* number one in our life? Do we put Christ first in our vacation plans, or do we try to get away from Him and backslide where no one will know us? Does He have first place in our business, or do we shave the truth and pilfer and cheat? Does He have first place in our home, or do we close the door on our godly behavior when we come home? Does He have first place in our thoughts and imaginations, or are we self-centered and introvert, thinking only of ourselves? "Casting down imaginations, and every high thing that exalteth itself against the knowledge of God, and bringing into captivity every thought to the obedience of Christ" (2 Co 10:5).

COLOSSIANS 1:19—"For it pleased the Father that in him should all fulness dwell."

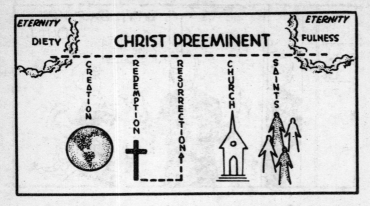

This reads literally, "For in him all the fullness of the Godhead was pleased to dwell," even as we read in Colossians 2:9, "For in him dwelleth all the fulness of the Godhead bodily."

He is the Head of the physical world; He was before nature and will be after nature; He is the Head of the supernatural world (Col 2:10); He is the Head of the church and of every individual saint *in Christ*. Since this is true, let us give Him His place.

He is the *fullness of God*. He is full of holiness, but we are full of sin; He is full of power, but we are full of weakness; He is full of love, but we are full of selfishness. How we need to let Him take over our lives! Can it be that we are robbing Him of His preeminence?

"And we know that the Son of God is come, and hath given us an understanding, that we may know him that is true, and we are in him that is true, even in his Son Jesus Christ. This is the true God [Christ is God], and

eternal life. Little children, keep yourselves from idols"
(1 Jn 5:20-21).

God's way is easy, for He is God!

QUESTIONS

1. Was Christ preexistent before creation? (Jn 17:5; 1 Jn 1:1)
2. Is Christ the Creator? (Jn 1:2-3; Heb 1:3, 10)
3. What is God's preknowledge and purpose? (Ro 8:28-30; Eph 1:4)
4. Is Christ called God? (Jn 20:28; Titus 2:13)
5. Did Christ accept worship? (Mt 14:33; 28:9)
6. Can man understand God's thoughts? (Ps 40:5; 139:6; Is 55:8-9)
7. God is the first and the last; is Christ the first and last? Rev 1:8, 17; 22:13)
8. Does Satan have a kingdom? (Jn 12:31; Eph 6:10-12)
9. Where is the Trinity associated as the three-in-one? (Gen 1:26-27; Mk 1:10-11; 2 Co 13:14)
10. How does one become a member of the church of Jesus Christ, the church universal? (Ac 2:47; 1 Co 10:32; Heb 12:23)

4

PEACE THROUGH CHRIST

Reconciliation and Its Results (Col 1:20-24)

SOMEONE SAID, "I don't see why I'm a sinner. I'm as good as anybody else!"

"Yes," I agreed, "You probably are, but everybody else is a sinner too! God says, 'There is none righteous, no, not one.'"

As this truth dawned upon that sin-blinded heart, and admission was made that there was need for the Saviour, then reconciliation and salvation followed, and contact with God was guaranteed. There is such a thing as the false tranquility of ignorance.

The word *reconciliation* means to become friends with an enemy, or to know harmony where there has been hostility. Man needs to be reconciled to God, to know peace instead of rebellion against God.

How Are Men Reconciled to God?

COLOSSIANS 1:20a—"And, having made peace through the blood of his cross, by him to reconcile all things unto himself."

This refers to peace with God, or salvation, when men who have become enemies against God by their sin may

63

accept His salvation and become saints and children of God. "Ye were without Christ, being aliens . . . and strangers . . . having no hope, and without God in the world: but now in Christ Jesus ye who sometimes [at one time] were far off are made nigh by the blood of Christ. For he is our peace. . . . For through him we both have access by one Spirit unto the Father. Now therefore ye are no more strangers and foreigners, but fellowcitizens with the saints, and of the household of God" (Eph 2:12-19).

God does not need to be reconciled to man; He has not been man's enemy. He offers peace to those who will accept His gift, for peace is for those who are at peace with Him.

The blood that was given upon the cross was given by the Lord of glory who "took upon him the form of a servant, and was made in the likeness of men: and being found in fashion as a man, he humbled himself, and be-

came obedient unto death, even the death of the cross"
(Phil 2:7-8). Even though He was fully God, He took
human frailties so that believers might be reconciled to
God "in the body of his flesh through death" (Col 1:22).

What Is the Extent of Reconciliation?

COLOSSIANS 1:20b—"To reconcile all things unto himself; by
him, I say, whether they be things in earth, or things in
heaven."

Things on earth would include nature's blights and
decay, the illnesses and death of animals, and the sin,
sickness and death of mankind, which are all the result
of God's curse upon sin.

Things in heaven refer to that which is in the first
heaven and the second heaven, but certainly not to that
within the third heaven, which is the place of the holy
presence of God. Things there need no reconciliation.

The first heaven is the atmosphere around our earth

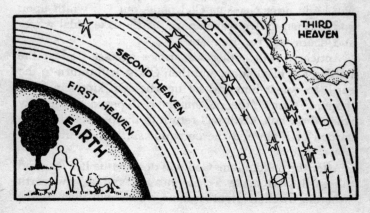

where bad weather and storms are a part of judgment upon sin. The second heaven includes the universe beyond where heavenly bodies (planets and meteorites, etc.) have been in a state of combustion, and some still are.

Reconciliation through the blood of Christ will lift this curse when He comes to earth for His millennial reign, and the whole system of nature will return to a perfect state.

Before continuing, let us take a quick look at God's plan for the future so we can better fit these events into the correct order.

We are now living in the church age which ends with the coming of Christ to catch away His church to glory (this is called the *rapture*) and then begins the seven years of the great tribulation on earth under the rule of Satan's counterfeit Christ, the Antichrist.

It is at the last part of this seven years that all nature will be in utter chaos as God pours out His wrath upon godless men. Then war, famine, earthquake, tidal waves and death will run rampant.

Antichrist will gather his armies against God at the Battle of Armageddon, and then Christ will return to the earth to defeat him and set up His own kingdom for a thousand years (the *millennium*) of peace and equity when the whole earth will return to the perfection of the garden of Eden and the curse for sin will be lifted (Is 35).

After the millennium, God will destroy the heavens and the earth and make a new heaven and a new earth "wherein dwelleth righteousness." This will then be the final reconciliation of all things. "That in the dispensation of the fulness of times he might gather together in one all things in Christ, both which are in heaven, and which are on earth; even in him" (Eph 1:10).

From Adam to the millennium, however, there is reconciliation only for those who receive God's way of salvation. Sickness, decay and death are still in the physical world, including the bodies of believers (Ro 8:18-23). The person (spirit and soul) of the saints is reconciled, but the body is still waiting for the perfection of a resurrection body.

Satan and his demons will never be reconciled; their destiny is the lake of fire (Mt 25:41).

Why Do Men Need to Be Reconciled?

COLOSSIANS 1:21—"And you that were sometime alienated and enemies in your mind by wicked works, yet now hath he reconciled."

Not only did Adam sin, and every human being ever since, but you and I have sinned too. We have turned our back upon God and chosen to serve *self* instead, and this amounts to our serving the devil. Satan is a hard taskmaster. Ask the man in prison, the drunkard and the dope addict. The one aim of the devil is to get even with God by keeping men from Him and damning them into the lake of fire with himself. He certainly works hard at it too.

Every one of us needs reconciliation because we have been rebellious against God and our works have been wicked. There are no exceptions. Remember the Quaker who confided to his friend, "Everyone is wrong except

me and thee, and sometimes me has me doubts about thee!" But when God says all have sinned, He means you, me and everybody else.

Wicked works are all things that are done that are contrary to the revealed will of God. If we get into collision with Him, then it is just too bad for us! But when man comes to the end of his rope, God steps in with the remedy, Jesus Christ, who came not only as a reformer and philosopher (though He was both), but as the Sin-bearer. So if anyone is to know reconciliation with Him, it must be on His terms, and this can be now— right now!

This comes close to home, doesn't it? You and I need to be reconciled. Have you accepted this Saviour as your way to peace with God? "We have peace with God through our Lord Jesus Christ" (Ro 5:1).

What Is the Result of Reconciliation?

COLOSSIANS 1:22—"In the body of his flesh through death, to present you holy and unblameable and unreproveable in his sight."

Reconciliation provided by the death of Christ is not just to make us happy. The ultimate purpose of God is to make us holy. All the created universe is but the scaffolding to set up the holy temple of God, the church. Perfection of holiness will be when we see the Lord, but in the meantime—if we are *in Christ*—God looks at us through Him, as it were, and we are accepted and counted holy even though we are not yet perfect. We are saints *in Christ* and this is our *positional holiness*. No wonder we can find that God's way is easy!

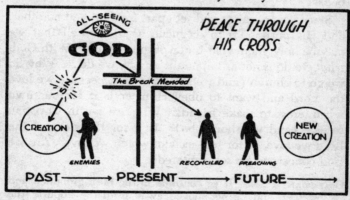

On the other hand, God also sees our behavior while we are here on earth, so this should be holy as well. This is *practical holiness*. The guarantee of future perfection is an incentive for practical holiness now under the all-seeing eye of God. He can see right through our sham and hyprocrisy, and knows when we pretend spirituality when we are not living it, and talk Christianity when we are really worldly. He sees all. "Neither is there any creature that is not manifest in his sight: but all things are naked and open unto the eyes of him with whom we have to do" (Heb 4:13). How this should put us on our mark!

In contrast though, it is a joy to know that when we are loving Him and living for Him and loving others to Him, He sees that too! "Your work of faith, and labour of love, and patience of hope in our Lord Jesus Christ, in the sight of God and our Father" (1 Th 1:3). God keeps the books!

Since we are saints and set apart for God and no other, and His purpose is to reconcile us to Himself that we may be holy, then what is our purpose in life? With God, *what* we do is not as important as *why* we do it. Why do we go to church (and we should)? Is it because we love the Lord and want to obey Him, or is it for our own self-interest to make friends? Why are we in Christian service (and we should be)? Is it for the glory of the Lord we love, or for self-acclaim which we love? Are we God-concerned or self-centered?

COLOSSIANS 1:23a—"If ye continue in the faith grounded and settled, and be not moved away from the hope of the gospel."

This is now the basis for God's approval and blessing and rewards. This is not now dealing with the matter of keeping our salvation, for that is the gift of God by faith *in Christ* and we do not earn that.

Scripture uses the word *faith* in several ways:

The *preaching of the faith*: this is the faith once delivered to the saints, the doctrine of Christ (Jude 3).

The *possession of faith*: the gift of God to those who receive Christ (Eph 2:8-9).

The *profession of faith*: witnessing for Christ (Ro 1:8).

The *practice of faith*: to be holy and unblameable in Christ (Ro 1:5).

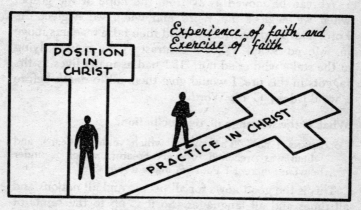

Continue in the faith—grounded on the foundation of our faith, Christ; settled in the doctrine of our faith, Christ! Here is the safeguard against backsliding. Settled! Not driven about by every wind of doctrine or every whisper of sin. The more we learn of the Lord and His Word, the more we will love Him because this is our daily diet and our delight. Or is it? We found during the war years that there is no strength in just remembering Christmas dinners of the past! When we returned to America after liberation from concentration camps, I remember how I hoarded every scrap of food when preparing meals; even celery tops were precious! My sister-in-law teased me, "You don't need to eat garbage now!"

Since then we've caught up on eating! But we will never catch up on feasting on the bread of life. It will always be our staple and should not be the less precious just because it is available and freely given.

We can be moved away from the hope of the gospel when we neglect the Word and when we neglect the Lord. Despondency follows and then false teachers move in. Moved away! What a contrast to the martyr dying at the stake who cried out, "If I had as many lives as the faggots in this fire, I would give them all to death before I would deny God's Word!"

What Is the Message of Reconciliation?

COLOSSIANS 1:23b—"The gospel, which ye have heard, and which was preached to every creature which is under heaven; whereof I Paul am made a minister."

This is the good news for all people and all nations and all times and all languages. So it is up to the saints of God to get this message out, for all are commissioned with the missionary message in these times. "And hath committed unto us the word of reconciliation. Now then we are ambassadors for Christ, as though God did beseech you by us: we pray you in Christ's stead, be ye reconciled to God" (2 Co 5:19-20). What are we doing about this?

Are we so bogged down in self-concern that we care nothing for others? God's way is easy for those who obey Him. What about us?

When asked, "Don't you tire of teaching doctrine and answering the same questions?" my reply was "How could I be tired of giving the gospel of hope to those that are without hope? Is a doctor bored when he has a cure for a suffering patient? Is a mother bored when she has a bottle of fresh formula for her hungry babe?"

A commercial artist and sports car enthusiast saw our lesson sheets and came to class just to "see what it was all about." He could not understand why anyone would go to study the Bible on a week night. That was only for Sundays!

Some weeks later that young man surrendered to Jesus Christ, as his wife had already done. Later they sold their home and enrolled in Bible school, and today they are home missionaries establishing new churches. How glad I am that we have the gospel to give out! Ambassadors for Christ!

The apostle Paul is not here today, but the message is here, and saints have the privilege of a "missionary calling" *in Christ*. It is not new teaching, not entertainment, not part truth, but the hope of the gospel!

"We shall be saved from wrath through him. For if, when we were enemies, we were reconciled to God by the death of his Son, much more, being reconciled, we shall be saved by his life [Christ ever lives to make intercession for us]. And not only so, but we also joy in God through our Lord Jesus Christ, by whom we have now received the atonement" (Ro 5:9-11).

God's way is easy!

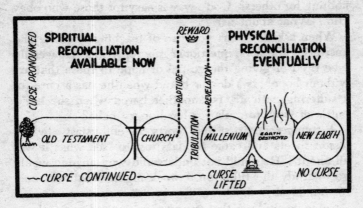

QUESTIONS

1. What is the condition of the lost? (Jer 17:9; Eph 2:12; 4:18-19)
2. When did God curse sin? (Gen 3)
3. When will the curse be lifted? (Mic 4:1-7; Rev 22:3)
4. How many men and women are guilty before God? (Is 53:6; Ro 3:9-23)
5. When will saints be perfect? (1 Th 3:13)
6. What is the best "grounding" for the believer? (Eph 3:17)
7. Where does Scripture teach about the rapture? (1 Co 15:51-57; 1 Th 4:16-18)
8. Where do we read about the great tribulation? (Mt 24:21; Rev 6-19)
9. Where are we taught about the millennium? (Rev 20:4-6)
10. Where are the new earth and heaven foretold? (2 Pe 3:10-13)

5

PROCLAIMING CHRIST

The Message and the Method (Col 1:24-29)

"I DON'T SEE WHY Mrs. Shorwod disagrees with so many people. I'm a Christian too, and yet I get along with everyone." The speaker was discussing a fine faithful Christian lady who gave a true witness for the Lord wherever she went.

"Are you actively witnessing?" I asked.

"Well, no," she admitted. "I keep quiet about my religion. I figure it's none of my business to set everyone straight."

"Then, my friend, that's why you have no opposition, and you probably don't have any converts either. You aren't showing your colors, so you're really playing on the enemy's team!"

She admitted that that was true.

How we enjoy the truth that we are saints *in Christ* and He is *in us*, but when it comes to martyrdom—that is something else!

The Martyrdom for Manifesting the Message

COLOSSIANS 1:24a—"Who now rejoice in my sufferings for you."

The message of the cross and martyrdom often go together, for a faithful witness is not going to be more popular than his Lord. "And thou shalt speak my words unto them, whether they will hear, or whether they will forbear" (Eze 2:7). It may mean loss of prestige or loss of a job, or less time for self or less pay. Seldom might a believer in our day be burned at the stake, but he often suffers over and over again in self-sacrifice and heartbreak.

The measure that we are willing to give up our plans and comforts in order to witness to others will be the measure of blessing, so this should be a good weapon against self-pity and a self-crowned halo!

Paul did not rejoice in suffering for suffering's sake. This was no self-inflicted penance and pain to gain acceptance with God, but this was the suffering that came because of his stand for Christ and that others might be saved. He suffered even as Moses suffered, "choosing rather to suffer affliction with the people of God, than to enjoy the pleasures of sin for a season" (Heb 11:25).

This attitude of Paul's is the example for all "sent saints." "For unto you it is given in the behalf of Christ, not only to believe on him, but also to suffer for his sake" (Phil 1:29). "That ye may be counted worthy of the kingdom of God, for which ye also suffer" (2 Th 1:5b). This is what Jesus meant when He said, "Whosoever will come after me, let him deny himself, and take up his cross, and follow me" (Mk 8:34b). How different this is to the carrying of a crucifix in a procession or on a chain

HOW MUCH HAVE WE SUFFERED?

around the neck! This refers to selfish denial. "If we suffer, we shall also reign with him: if we deny him, he also will deny us" (2 Ti 2:12).

COLOSSIANS 1:24b—"And fill up that which is behind of the afflictions of Christ in my flesh for his body's sake, which is the church."

What does this mean? Did Christ lack in His sufferings for us? Of course not! But Paul realized that he lacked in suffering compared to Christ, and that he could never catch up, no matter how much he endured or labored. He was willing to suffer, if need be, to show his gratitude to Christ as well as to witness to others.

On first thought it seems that Paul endured more trials than any other (2 Co 11), for he suffered beatings, stonings and imprisonments and was even left as dead three times. He had a physical handicap and was eventually beheaded in Rome. Then how did he come behind compared to Christ?

The answer is clear. Christ is God! The all-holy, eternal One of glory became the poorest of men, the most despised, and "made himself of no reputation, and took upon him the form of a servant, and was made in the likeness of men . . . he humbled himself, and became obedient unto death, even the death of the cross" (Phil 2:7-8).

Jesus' sufferings far exceeded Paul's, and Paul's exceed ours, so how can we ever begin to think that we know what persecution is? The fear of suffering stems right back to our old enemy, *self*. We hesitate to lend ourselves because it might cost us something of self-denial; we fear to grow for God because it might mean that we will be called to go for God.

The Minister to Manifest the Message

Colossians 1:25—"Whereof I am made a minister, according to the dispensation of God which is given to me for you, to fulfil the word of God."

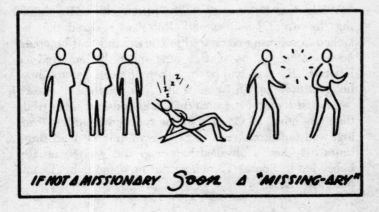

IF NOT A MISSIONARY *Soon* A "MISSING-ARY"

Paul is not here now, so men and women are needed to fall into line to carry the message. Any Christian who is not a missionary will soon be missing—missing in blessing and usefulness! For this task of giving forth God's truth is now given to all saints in order that we might obey and bear the Word to accomplish that which He pleases.

Paul had a unique dispensation of God in the privilege of giving and writing newly revealed truth and thus completing the Scriptures. So his fulfilling the Word of God would also apply to his completing it and "filling it full" as far as inspired revelation is concerned. This we do not claim for ourselves. But we can claim the privilege of knowing and growing and glowing and going with the Word of God!

Each believer *in Christ* can fulfill the Word of God when he puts it into practice. That which He has given we are to work out like a mathematical problem given to a student. "Work out your own salvation with fear and trembling. For it is God which worketh in you both to will and to do of his good pleasure" (Phil 2:12-13). We do not *work for* our salvation, but God helps us *work it out* in practice. This makes God's way easy.

The Mystery of the Message

COLOSSIANS 1:26—"Even the mystery which hath been hid from ages and from generations, but now is made manifest to his saints."

Have you ever watched a magician perform and wondered how he worked his amazing tricks? They were mystifying because you did not know how they were done, but to the magician they were simple enough and no mystery. So it is with some of the truths of the Word of God. They are as clear as the mind of God Himself, but some of them were only revealed for the first time through the apostle Paul.

A *mystery* in Bible terms is simply a truth newly revealed. It is not new, but newly given. It is as old as eternal God. As Paul said, "According to my gospel, and the preaching of Jesus Christ, according to the revelation of the mystery, which was kept secret since the world began, but now is made manifest, and by the scriptures of the prophets, according to the commandment of the everlasting God, made known to all nations for the obedience of faith" (Ro 16:25-26).

Throughout past ages men did not have full revelation from God. It was hidden in the complex rituals of the tabernacle and temple worship which were types of the coming Lamb of God. Now there emerges from them the

shining clearness of the Lamb of God who did come and whose Spirit now indwells the saints *in Christ*.

Through the apostle Paul and the Spirit of Christ, the message is now given to all the saints. This is not just for the clergy. "Be ready always to give an answer to every man that asketh you a reason of the hope that is in you" (1 Pe 3:15). To witness is to know something and tell it.

The Message Manifested

Colossians 1:27—"To whom God would make known what is the riches of the glory of this mystery among the Gentiles; which is Christ in you, the hope of glory."

Here it is! This is the message: "Christ in you!" The gospel changes from a Jewish sect to a worldwide opportunity, and all barriers are down so that Jew and Gentile saints alike are fellow heirs with Christ because He is *in them*. "For he is our peace, who hath made both one, and hath broken down the middle wall of partition between us . . . for to make in himself of twain one new man, so making peace" (Eph 2:14-15). A Gentile is anyone who is not a Jew.

Up to now the emphasis of the book of Colossians has been that the saints are *in Christ*. Now we have the counterpart: Christ is also *in them*. "What? Know ye not that your body is the temple of the Holy Ghost which is in you?" (1 Co 6:19). Remember, though, that this is the *Holy* Spirit, the Spirit of holiness, the Spirit of Christ and the Spirit of God. "Know ye not that ye are the temple of God, and that the Spirit of God dwelleth in you?" (1 Co 3:16). He must begin by cleaning house.

We once lived in a bamboo hut that belonged to a

witch doctor while we were on the mission field in the Philippines. He had left his shrine and fetish (in case we might like to use them!) but took the corn and tobacco that had been drying from the rafters, and the livestock which lived in the barnyard under the house. Of course, they also left the family cemetery which was also under the house, plus the pig mire, corn bugs, cockroaches and bedbugs!

We moved in, but we had to rearrange things somewhat! We scrubbed and repaired, and we tried to scour off the betel-nut juice that had been chewed and spat all over the floor and walls. Then we filled in the pig slough and the sinking graves. If this was to be our home, it had to be cleaned up!

Can we expect less for the Lord of glory when He comes to take over our heart? Can we deny His cleaning house? Do the vermin of self-esteem and the bugs of self-seeking need spraying with God's insecticide of holiness? Does that slough of jealousy need filling in with His love and grace? "Christ in you, the hope of glory!"

Without Him we are empty, helpless, hopeless—nothing! "For without me ye can do nothing" (Jn 15:5). We are even less than nothing. Zero is bad enough, but minus zero is worse! "All nations before him are as nothing; and they are counted to him less than nothing, and vanity" (Is 40:17). Thank God, this does not mean that He considers us as nothing, but that, in comparison to Him, we are less than nothing.

"Christ in you, the hope of glory!" The future is a hope and not a dread. Bereavement loses its despair, and death loses its sting. "In hope of eternal life, which God, that

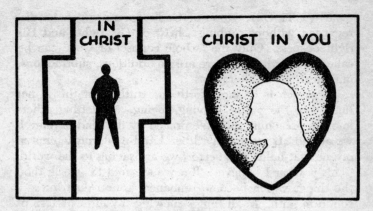

cannot lie, promised before the world began" (Titus 1:2). *Hope* is a powerful word. "Patience of hope in our Lord Jesus Christ. . . . Knowing, brethren beloved, your election of God" (1 Th 1:3-4). This is the message, the mystery.

The Means of Manifesting the Message

COLOSSIANS 1:28a—"Whom we preach, warning every man, and teaching every man in all wisdom."

This is the "ways and means department," the how-to-do-it part of the message. Notice it does not say *what* we preach, but *whom*. We do not offer to the world a biography of a great leader; we preach Christ! We do not offer rituals and rules to lost souls; we preach Christ! We do not work miracles; we preach Christ! "Teach no other doctrine, neither give heed to fables" (1 Ti 1:3-4). "Preach the word; be instant in season, out of season; reprove, rebuke, exhort with all longsuffering and doctrine" (2 Ti 4:2). None of God's doctrines can be disregarded without robbing Christ of His rights and His righteousness. Only the "whole counsel of God" can be called the truth, and there are no additions, subtractions, modifications or alterations.

To preach is to show forth the truth. But this is not limited to the pulpit. Living, loving, and letting others know is preaching too. We preach by the kind of church we attend. If we are in a liberal and modernistic church or one that holds some error, we are saying to the world, "This is what I believe!" But we are told to "speak thou the things which become [enhance] sound doctrine . . . sound in faith. In all things shewing thyself a pattern of good works: in doctrine shewing uncorruptness, gravity, sincerity, sound speech, that cannot be condemned" (Titus 2:1-2, 7-8).

However, the gospel is not all positive blessing; there is also warning against side-stepping the truth just because it might be unpopular or controversial. Remember, the Bible is always controversial when men are not right with God.

A lady said, "You said something that hit my religion!"

"Is what I said in the Bible?" I asked her. "Did you follow in your Bible as I was reading?"

"Yes, it did say that all right."

"Well, I didn't make it up," I reminded her. "This is God's Word!"

Preaching by lip or by life includes warning. It must be the truth, the whole truth, and nothing but the truth—but truth given in love.

Preaching pours out the truth, as it were, but teaching

digs it in! Preaching persuades men, but teaching makes them understand. "So they read in the book in the law of God distinctly, and gave the sense, and caused them to understand the reading" (Neh 8:8).

This has been the endeavor in our missionary work both on the foreign field and here at home in America—

Bible-teaching evangelism. In the Philippines we set up large tents and stayed right on location week after week until the Lord gave a harvest of souls. It meant toil, tears, sweat, and difficult living in a trailer, much prayer and visiting and, most of all, teaching, teaching, teaching! Today there are many fine Bible-believing churches which were begun and Christian workers who came to Christ during those long-term campaigns.

The same principle is true in the Bible classes here in America. Those who come to Christ are the ones who understand something of the doctrines of God, and then they come into a sound Bible-teaching church to serve the Lord.

As far as personal witnessing to lead a soul to Christ, the four basic steps that have been used for many years are still good:

1. Show the need for the Saviour—all are sinners and condemned (Ro 3:23; 6:23; Rev 20:15; 21:8).
2. Show that Christ alone is the Saviour (Jn 3:16; Ro 5:8).
3. Show how to receive the Saviour (Jn 1:12; Ro 10:13; Rev 3:20).
4. Show how to be sure of salvation (Jn 3:36; 10:27-30; 1 Jn 5:12-13).

An even more simple method to lead a person to decision to receive the Saviour is to limit the conversation to John 3:16 alone:

1. Show the need for the Saviour ("perish" is for those who do not receive Him).
2. Show Christ the Saviour ("God . . . gave his only begotten Son").
3. Show how to receive the Saviour ("believeth" means more than just to believe about Him; it means to receive Him personally).
4. Show how to be sure of salvation ("should not perish, but have everlasting life").

This preaching is for every saint *in Christ*, the average Christian. Try reading the Bible with the neighbor who drops in for coffee; pray with a worried friend; read a portion of Scripture and have a short prayer with dinner guests (no matter who they are!); give a testimony of what the Lord means to you in any casual conversation or on the telephone.

The Motive for Manifesting the Message

COLOSSIANS 1:28b—"That we may present every man perfect in Christ Jesus."

"Perfect" means to be mature, complete and fully grown, to "continue to grow" to victory. Too many new converts do not grow because they do not know. This is the meaning of "Christ in you, the hope of glory"—the going on to spiritual maturity and godliness. There is no shortcut to victory, and maturity is not won in a moment, but God will work in us if we but let Him have His place as the Head. However, even a new Christian can be a spiritual Christian, completely filled with the desire for His will. This does not take maturity, only willingness!

"Why don't I ever have any converts?" a man asked me.

"Only God wins converts," I reminded him. "But what are you doing to reach people?"

"Nothing much. I'm waiting for God to bring someone to me to be saved." Poor fellow, he might have to wait forever!

Witnessing is a battle against the self-will of sin-ridden hearts, the wrestling against the wickedness of Satan's demons, the opposition of errors that springs up, and the indifference of backslidden Christians who are stumbling

blocks. It's a real battle in which the worst enemies are our own selfishness and indifference!

COLOSSIANS 1:29—"Whereunto I also labour, striving according to his working, which worketh in me mightily."

There must be honest effort if there is to be a harvest, for there is no progress without perspiration! Spiritual harvest begins by plowing the fallow ground by preaching, planting the seeds by teaching, cultivating by love, watering by prayer, and weeding by rebuke and warning. This is indeed a labor of love! But it is a privilege, not a privation!

All effective preaching, teaching, warning and labor are the work of God *through* the saint that is *in Christ*. He "worketh in me mightily." This should be a stoplight against our being tempted to steal any of the glory from the Lord, for our physical efforts do not produce true spiritual fruit; it is His doing. Even as salvation is completely due to His grace, so true success in service is the result of His grace. So hands off, Christian, hands off the glory!

How eager we are to snatch at the bouquets, but we shrink at the thorns hidden among the roses! Ministry? Yes! Martyrdom? No!

"When ye do well, and suffer for it, ye take it patiently, this is acceptable with God. For even hereunto were ye called: because Christ also suffered for us, leaving us an example, that ye should follow his steps" (1 Pe 2:20b-21).

QUESTIONS

1. What relevance do Christ's sufferings have for Christians? (Heb 12:3; 1 Pe 2:20-21)
2. How should the saints react toward suffering? (Ja 1:2-4, 12; 1 Pe 3:14-17; 4:16, 19)
3. What did Jesus say about completing the Old Testament? (Mt 5:17-18)
4. Did the Old Testament saints understand all the gospel? (1 Pe 1:9-12)
5. What are some of the "mysteries" in the epistles? (Ro 11:25; 1 Co 2:7; 4:1; 15:51; Eph 1:9; 3:3-4, 19)
6. Who is the temple of God? (1 Co 3:16-17)
7. What is the message of the saints? (1 Co 1:23; 2 Co 4:5)
8. Does God command Christians to teach? (1 Ti 1:3; 4:11; 6:2; 2 Ti 2:2)
9. What is the incentive to labor for the Lord? (1 Co 3:9; 15:57; 1 Th 2:9)
10. Does God allow His saints to suffer? (2 Co 11:23-33)

6

PROGRESS IN CHRIST
Warning and Walking (Col 2:1-10)

HAVE YOU EVER CONSIDERED how fortunate we are to have whole libraries of Christian literature available to us? In Paul's time how the believers must have cherished his few letters, and how often they must have read and re-read them!

"I can't afford to buy books. I need my money to feed my family!" said a Christian when encouraged to buy a pamphlet for home Bible study. But only a short time

What reading material do we buy?

later she came out of the supermarket with an armful of groceries *and* a sheaf of the latest popular magazines under her arm!

Warfare

COLOSSIANS 2:1—"For I would that ye knew what great conflict I have for you, and for them at Laodicea, and for as many as have not seen my face in the flesh."

Paul was not only writing to those in his time, but to us who have not seen his face in the flesh. His burden was for saints to be strong in doctrine and not easily shaken. It costs something to stand up and be counted and be unpopular, for human wisdom says, "Keep an open mind! Don't be dogmatic! There's good in all religions!" But God says just the opposite. "Earnestly contend for the faith which was once delivered unto the saints" (Jude 3b). This is no spiritual pacifism! Service that counts, costs. Unlike Paul, we are so often so occupied and full of ourselves that we have no time or care for others, to wrestle in prayer for them, that they be victorious against the attacks of the devil. In our time Satan is not only trying to get men to deny God and sin, he even goes so far as to get them to deny there is a devil! How's that for a trick? Some who pride themselves in mental prowess hold Satan-inspired theories, such as: the devil is only principle, for there is no personal Satan; when the Bible speaks about the devil, it only means weak human beings; sinful actions are the only devil we have to contend against; there is no devil, sin, sickness, death or hell; just dismiss such ideas from your mind!

The absurdity of such vain speculation is pathetic, for

these vain thinkers still have locks on their doors, and tombstones mark their graves.

Welfare

COLOSSIANS 2:2a—"That their hearts might be comforted, being knit together in love."

This comfort is not soothing syrup, but rather strength by companionship, and power to resist sin and error. The Holy Spirit is the Comforter to go alongside to help and "to establish you, and to comfort you concerning your faith" (1 Th 3:2). There is no real comfort or strength apart from the Spirit and the Word of God. When we let God take over our minds and opinions which we once used for the devil, we turn the guns back on our enemy!

KNIT TOGETHER

LOVE

The Fruit of the Spirit.

Love is overwhelming adoration for the Lord that produces genuine concern for the well-being of others. Thus, love is a weapon for victory. "Looking diligently lest any man fail of the grace of God [fail to live graciously before

God]; lest any root of bitterness springing up trouble you, and thereby many be defiled" (Heb 12:15). Of course, this spiritual love and unity can only be if there is no compromise with error in doctrine or practice, which we are to oppose.

What does it mean to be knit together in love? When very young, I admired an older girl who had her broken arm in a cast. I thought it was beautiful! She told me proudly, "My arm is knitting now!" My eyes grew big, and I wondered how they got knitting needles inside that cast! I didn't understand that the bones were growing together—knitting together. This is God's will for the saints *in Christ*—that they might be strong for the warfare. *On* the truth of God, *in* the will of God, *by* the power of God and *for* the glory of God, believers are united.

COLOSSIANS 2:2b—"Unto all riches of the full assurance of understanding."

This is another weapon for victory: assurance of understanding. Have you noticed how often the book of Colossians touches on the importance of spiritual wisdom and knowledge? Paul was concerned that the seed sown would not be smothered by weeds of doubt and quarrels and men's philosophies. It is not enough to sow good seed; it is also necessary to pull out the weeds.

No doubt there was some persuasive leader in Colosse who was challenging the gospel Epaphras had preached, and with oratory and human intellectualism he was endangering the faith of the saints.

Colossians 2:2c—"To the acknowledgement of the mystery of God, and of the Father, and of Christ." (Note: The last phrase is not found in the best manuscripts.)

The ultimate of human search is that the saints be filled with the knowledge of the will and message of God, which is "Christ in you, the hope of glory." This is the mystery of God—truth not revealed before, but now made clear—Christ is the fullness of the Godhead, and He embodies all wisdom and knowledge for the redemption of man. We can never comprehend all the riches of His wisdom, but we can understand what we need to know and what God has given in His Word. "But of him are ye in Christ Jesus, who of God is made unto us wisdom, and righteousness, and sanctification, and redemption: that, according as it is written, He that glorieth, let him glory in the Lord" (1 Co 1:30-31).

Colossians 2:3—"In whom are hid all the treasures of wisdom and knowledge."

DIG OUT GOD'S GEMS

Spiritual wisdom is completely buried as far as the unsaved man is concerned. "Neither can he know them, because they are spiritually discerned" (1 Co 2:14). But the believers will want to dig out these hidden truths. The word "hid" does not mean that they can never be found, but rather that they are there to be discovered.

The Bible will give us a lifetime of digging out nuggets of gold and acres of diamonds which are not found by going to church just once a week. To dig is to read regularly and eagerly, apply and obey, comparing scripture with scripture. "That the God of our Lord Jesus Christ, the Father of glory, may give unto you the spirit of wisdom and revelation in the knowledge of him" (Eph 1:17).

Warning

COLOSSIANS 2:4—"And this I say, lest any man should beguile you with enticing words."

"Beguile" in this context has the meaning of twisting the truth and enticing into error. Whoever the false teacher was (he might have been the one Paul mentions in Acts 20:29-30), he was evidently eloquent and persuasive, with an outward form of humility and an overdose of confused doctrine. To summarize some of the false teaching: Christ is just one in a long line of mediators; all matter is evil; human wisdom is exalted; Judaism is carried over; angelic powers are revered; and there is contempt for the physical body.

God warns, "Teach no other doctrine, neither give heed to fables" (1 Ti 1:3-4). Fluent oratory, magnetic personality, excellent logic, hypnotic persuasion and fine rhetoric might all be good in themselves, but they become the devil's tools when they are used by skeptics and false teachers. For enticing words often are close to the truth, yet any teaching that has even one wrong doctrine is Satan-inspired.

Walking

COLOSSIANS 2:5—"For though I be absent in the flesh, yet am I with you in the spirit, joying and beholding your order, and the stedfastness of your faith in Christ."

To be present in the spirit is to be thinking and praying and yearning for the spiritual strength of the Colossian Christians. How often the excuse that they are there in spirit is given today by those who stay away from church or prayer meeting! However, it is not too inspiring to a pastor to have a room full of spirits! But Paul was in a Roman prison, so he could legitimately be excused from being present in the flesh!

God is the Author of order who ordained church leadership and financial matters as well as discipline. "Let all things be done decently and in order" (1 Co 14:40). The Christians at Colosse had indeed been well taught by Epaphras and were orderly in their assemblies (in contrast to Corinthians who were falling into confusion), and this brought joy to Paul the prisoner.

Once again we come to the words "faith in Christ." Up to then the saints had not succumbed to the onslaught of error but were steadfast in the truth that produced faith. God says, "And ye shall seek me, and find me, when ye shall search for me with all your heart. And I will be found of you, saith the LORD" (Jer 29:13-14). This is the place to avoid error, and this is the place to know God's way is easy.

Faith is trust in God for salvation from hell, for victory in life, for eternity in glory. To have faith is to lean our spiritual weight upon Him in sorrow or in joy, in sickness or in health, until death takes us into His presence in heaven!

Why not trust the sign?

A traveler lost in a blizzard could not find the bridge to cross the river near his home. Because he did not know if the ice was strong enough to carry his weight, he crawled tremblingly on hands and knees, listening for any sound of cracking ice. Then he heard singing. A farmer was driving a four-horse load of coal across the ice and singing as he went! The farmer knew and trusted himself to the ice.

We can trust the Almighty to carry us and our burdens as well, and a little singing along the way would not hurt either!

COLOSSIANS 2:6—"As ye have therefore received Christ Jesus the Lord, so walk ye in him."

Often, when asked when they received the Saviour, people mumble, "Well, I think— It must have been— I'm not sure. I don't remember!" Why not know the date? This is the most important day in our life, far more so than our birthday or wedding day.

To receive Christ is the moment of praying and asking Him to come into our life and take our sin away. This is the once-for-all-time and once-forever day of decision, our salvation day, our spiritual birthday into God's family. It is the hour when we are placed in Christ and become saved, sanctified and safe! What could be more important than that? "That if thou shalt confess with thy mouth the Lord Jesus, and shalt believe in thine heart . . . thou shalt be saved" (Ro 10:9). "But as many as received him, to them gave he power to become the sons of God, even to them that believe on his name" (Jn 1:12). If there is

IN STEP!

any doubt at all about this date, now is the time to settle it. Right now!

To "walk in him" is to think and act in step with Christ. This is progress and not just activity. How did Christ walk? He so loved that He gave Himself, and He came to seek and to save that which was lost. He spent time in prayer, and He was in God's house regularly. He knew and used the Scriptures; He was baptized, and He was holy. This is how He walked! You see, walking as He walked is another term for good works. "They which have believed in God might be careful to maintain good works" (Titus 3:8; see also 1 Jn 2:6).

COLOSSIANS 2:7a—"Rooted and built up in him."

Here again are the words "in him." Believers must be in Him before they can grow and walk like Him. Faith in Him is like the roots in the ground; the deeper the roots, the higher the tree can rise. Also, the growing tree will bear the same characteristics as the root, so that the bark, branches, leaves and fruit will all be of the same kind. As the tree takes nourishment from the roots, so the saints *in Christ* receive spiritual strength from Him. You will never find walnuts on a banana tree or apples on a rosebush! Christlike character comes from being planted in the good soil of salvation *in Christ*, with His spiritual life flowing through us to make God's way easy.

The outreach of the branches also depends on the depth of the roots. So the deeper we are involved with the Lord in reading His Word, learning about Him, and loving and obeying Him, the greater the outreach to others with the gospel.

COLOSSIANS 2:7b—"And established in the faith, as ye have been taught."

There is no getting away from the word "faith," is there? In this instance it is referring to the doctrine of God that is to stablish the saints so they may be steadfast and grow.

"As ye have been taught" does not mean that men must remain in the same religion of their childhood. Anything but that! Just because a man is a horse thief does not mean that he must stay a horse thief! Paul is referring here to the truth which Epaphras had taught the Christians in Colosse, which was the gospel Paul taught, and which all saints have to teach now. (See Ac 16:5; 2 Th 2:16-17.)

A man said, "I don't dare study the Bible. It might turn me away from my church. I was baptized into this religion, and I'm afraid to change now!"

There is but one answer: "You do not dare to reject the Word of God. You'd better let Him determine your beliefs, no matter what you were raised to believe."

On the other hand, some Christians who do know the Scriptures, fall into the snare of being cold and bored with the treasures of wisdom and knowledge of Christ. This is like the woman on a sightseeing bus through the Grand Canyon, who sat reading a magazine while everyone else was exclaiming over the view. When asked why she did not look up, she yawned. "Oh, I've been here before!" she said.

COLOSSIANS 2:7c—"Abounding therein with thanksgiving."

This is both a weapon for victory over error as well as the fruit of being *in Christ*. Thanksgiving includes holiness and service which is to abound (leap over its bounds!) with the *word* and *work*. These must go together, for the *word* alone might give spiritual dispepsia, and *work* alone is powerless and futile effort.

Warning Again!

COLOSSIANS 2:8a—"Beware lest any man spoil you through philosophy and vain deceit."

Paul resumes his warnings. "Philosophy" means the "love of knowledge" (excellent in itself), but there is good and bad philosophy. This is now speaking of the bad. This is the imagination of Satan-enslaved minds that sows weeds alongside the tree of faith.

To "spoil" has the meaning of "take captive and rob." Beware, Christians! Let nothing strip us of our effectiveness and fruitfulness by deviating from the truth, and let no one rob us of our reward in glory either. John said, "Look to yourselves, that we lose not those things which we have wrought, but that we receive a full reward" (2 Jn 8).

How can we lose our reward? To worship and work under a church that is not based 100 percent on the truth is indeed to fly under the wrong flag. "If there come any unto you, and bring not this doctrine, receive him not into your house [to listen to his teachings], neither bid him God speed [wish him well]: for he that biddeth him God speed is partaker of his evil deeds [and will be judged with false teachers]" (2 Jn 10-11).

COLOSSIANS 2:8b—"After the tradition of men, after the rudiments of the world, and not after Christ."

This is the dividing point between truth and error, either in obedience to Christ, or not after Christ. God never changes His mind, so we had better fit in with Him! The sad fact in Colossians is that these warnings were not given to outsiders but to wavering Christians. They were to be on guard against false doctrine.

Does this fit into the situation of our times? Yes, for errors are even more prevalent now than ever before.

Beware of the "social gospel" which is humanism (self-effort and reform without salvation), and "humanitarianism" (social service without salvation) which has taken hold on modern churches in a new thrust.

Beware of "gnosticism" (no one can know anything for sure). Such contend that "we have no breakthrough to understand the infinite. We are all incomplete!" They are incomplete all right; they are without God! Others say, "Unless we can understand a matter, it cannot be so!" They are living in the kingdom of "don't know" and really do not want to know. They would rather flounder in empty ignorance of God than believe His Word. How the devil must rejoice over so-called "free thinkers" who are really thinking his thoughts after him! He was dangerous in Paul's time, but since then he has had two thousand years more to practice!

Beware of "modernism" (departing from the faith) which is as old as the garden of Eden with its challenge of the Word of God, and as vicious as the Jews who challenged the deity of Christ, and as wicked as the demons who deny the message of the blood of Christ. Modernists are found in many denominations today, but they are not always easy to distinguish, for they use Bible words with a human meaning. They speak of the "Master," meaning that Jesus was only a great leader, the death of Christ being a supreme martyrdom, heaven is here on earth, that all men are brothers under God (the Fatherhood of God and the brotherhood of man).

These twentieth-century philosophers have turned deliberately from the known truth and therefore are far worse than cults and errors which have sprung up from ignorance of God's Word. Jesus' words to the lawyers were: "Ye have taken away the key of knowledge; ye entered not in yourselves, and them that were entering in ye hindered" (Lk 11:52). How up to date the Bible is!

Liberal modernistic churches are the ones that are propagating the union of all churches, but those that are true to the Word will never unite with those which have error. Remember, the devil believes that Christ is God,

and demons go to church too (Mk 1:23), but not to worship!

These are the dandelions, thistles and crabgrass that threaten to smother the tree that is bearing fruit *in Christ*.

Beware of the teaching which says that only the parts of the Bible that meet your need are inspired; this is a turning from the *verbal inspiration* of Scripture. It moderates the strict stand of the Bible and tries to update it by condoning worldliness; this is a turning from the *doctrine* of the Scripture. It believes everyone should hold hands in evangelistic efforts, regardless of doctrinal stand; this is a turning from the *separation* of the Scripture. Its morals are relative to that which custom and environment and society sanction; this is a turning from the *moral stand* of the Scripture. But what does God say? "Now we command you, brethren, in the name of our Lord Jesus Christ, that ye withdraw yourselves from every brother that walketh disorderly, and not after the tradition which he received of us" (2 Th 3:6).

"Rudiments of the world" include any thought or teaching that rejects or neglects or modifies or bypasses the doctrine of Christ—rationalism, traditionalism, humanism, worldliness and personal preference ahead of Christ. "Do ye not therefore err, because ye know not the scriptures, neither the power of God?" (Mk 12:24).

The fundamental doctrines of the Bible have not changed for two thousand years. These are the basic truths upon which there is no choice, such as the verbal inspiration of the Scriptures (that every word in the original manuscripts was inspired of God); the triune God (God the Father, God the Son, and God the Spirit are all fully God); the depravity of man (all have sinned); salvation by faith (only by faith in Christ as the Sin-bearer); faith produces good works (works do not aid salvation); there is a heaven and there is a hell; the saints *in Christ* are saved forever and for sure (the security of the believer).

Worship

COLOSSIANS 2:9—"For in him dwelleth all the fulness of the Godhead bodily."

Worship is the heart occupied with the Son of God. It is information and understanding of God which results in affection, appreciation and response in obedience. Worship is focused on our Lord Jesus Christ in whom all the Trinity is pleased to dwell. There can be no worship until we have adored Him, and no service until we have worshiped. In prayer our minds are occupied with our needs; in praise we are occupied with our blessings; in service we are occupied with other people; but in worship we are occupied with God Himself!

COLOSSIANS 2:10—"And ye are complete in him, which is the head of all principality and power."

All that we need for time and eternity is placed in our account when we receive Him, for then we are complete *in Him*. All that is needed is to grow! And grow we must,

or else we remain babies forever. Every new Christian has the potential to grow up in the Lord and to be a strong man, a wise man and a godly man.

A handsome man sat across from us at a lunch counter. He had a fascinating profile and luxurious hair. But when he stepped down to leave the counter, everyone looked in amazement and pity. He was only three feet tall, and his deformed body limped away in slow painful steps. That deformity was no fault of his own at all, but it did remind me of this truth regarding Christ, our Head, and the body, His church. Are we as saintlike in practice as our position *in Christ?* His will is "that ye may stand perfect and complete in all the will of God" (Col 4:12b).

Someone complains, "Then why doesn't God make me good?"

The answer is that we very often do not really want to be made good. We have a responsible will and must choose purity even as we chose to accept salvation. We are free to do as we please just as long as we please the Lord. "Where the Spirit of the Lord is, there is liberty" (2 Co 3:17b). This is liberty to live for God, to be victorious over sin, and to win others to Him. Instead, are we hobbling around on crutches spiritually and just "getting along" and being satisfied with that? God wants us to grow!

The Head of the angel principalities and powers and the Head of all creation and the Head of the church is

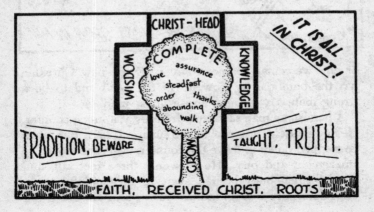

the One who has completed our salvation from damnation, and therefore will complete our perfection in glory. What a magnificent Head He is!

But are we, who are His body, as glorious as our Head? "Christ also loved the church, and gave himself for it; that he might sanctify and cleanse it . . . that he might present it to himself a glorious church" (Eph 5:25-27).

God's way is easy!

QUESTIONS

1. Should Christians fight for the truth? (1 Ti 6:12; 2 Ti 4:7)
2. Is there a personal devil? (Mt 13:19; 1 Pe 5:8)
3. What information is given about the devil? (Ac 26:18; 1 Jn 3:8)
4. Do some turn from the truth? (2 Ti 4:3-4; 2 Pe 1:16)
5. What does God instruct about order? (Ac 21:24; Titus 1:5)
6. Are believing and trust the same for the Old and New Testaments? (Ps 112:7; Eph 1:12-13; 1 Ti 4:10)
7. What is the basis of belief? (Ac 17:11-12; 1 Co 2:12)
8. How does God establish the saints? (Ro 1:11; 2 Co 1:21; Jas 5:8; 1 Pe 5:10; 2 Pe 1:12)
9. What does God think of the traditions invented by men? (Mt 15:3; Gal 1:14; 1 Pe 1:18)
10. What does God say about separation from error and false teachers? (Ro 16:17-18; 1 Co 5:9-13; 2 Co 6:14-17; 2 Th 3:6, 14-15; 1 Jn 4:1-6; Jude 3-4)

7

PICTURING SALVATION IN CHRIST

Circumcision, Baptism, Salvation (Col 2:11-13)

THE BIBLE PAINTS PICTURES in words and types to illustrate God's plan of salvation. Long before the Saviour actually came, godly men looked forward to the coming holy One, even as we now look back to His coming and look forward to His second coming. The Old Testament is a commentary on the New, and the New Testament is a commentary on the Old. We cannot take one without the other.

It is well to remind ourselves that the Old Testament laws were given primarily to the children of Abraham through Isaac, and were not given to Christians in the church age—unless they are carried over and repeated for us after the death of Christ. For example, God never commands Christians not to eat pork or other foods forbidden to the Jews. In fact, we are told, "Every creature of God is good, and nothing to be refused, if it be received with thanksgiving" (1 Ti 4:4). Since we cannot give thanks for poisonous foods, we do not eat them! I know that we were mighty grateful for the cat we caught in the prison camp when our children were starving, and we gave thanks for that meal! But we are not giving thanks for and eating cat meat today!

Neither does God command Christians to keep the Jewish Sabbath. This was given as a distinguishing sign to show God's special covenant with them as His chosen earthly people.

In Paul's time there was the problem of the transition from the laws given through Moses and the advanced Christian truth given through Paul and John for this new dispensation. Many of the Christian Jews still thought that Gentile converts had to become Jews if they were to be counted Christians (Ac 15).

Jesus lived under the age of law (of the tribe of Judah), but at His death and resurrection the new covenant (the New Testament) was established. Instead of human priests and physical types, we now have access to God through Christ as our High Priest, and every believer is

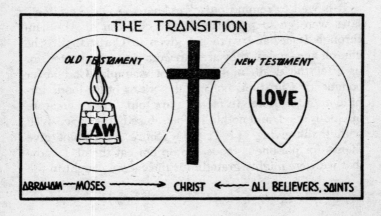

a priest unto God to offer up spiritual sacrifices of prayer, praise, holiness and service. "Ye also, as lively [living] stones, are built up a spiritual house, an holy priesthood, to offer up spiritual sacrifices, acceptable unto God by Jesus Christ" (1 Pe 2:5).

Circumcision

COLOSSIANS 2:11a—"In whom also ye are circumcised with the circumcision made without hands."

When God called Abraham and promised to make of him a great nation, He gave him a sign to separate his descendants from the heathen peoples. This sign was the physical operation of circumcision administered to every male child eight days after birth as an initiation ceremony showing that he belonged to the chosen race. It had nothing to do with spiritual salvation, for all the Jews certainly were not godly persons.

Today physical circumcision is merely practiced as a health measure, and it has not been given to Christians as a sign. Abraham was saved by faith, just as believers are in this age. "Faith was reckoned to Abraham for righteousness. How was it then reckoned? When he was in circumcision [after he was circumcised], or in uncircumcision? Not in circumcision, but in uncircumcision. And he received the sign of circumcision, a seal of the righteousness of the faith which he had yet being uncircumcised: that he might be the father of all them that believe, though they be not circumcised; that righteousness might be imputed [put to their account] unto them also" (Ro 4:9b-11).

Therefore, circumcision and the keeping of the sabbath and all the rest of the Old Testament laws come under the heading of "law works" for Israel.

In Colossians the rite of circumcision is used as an illustration of spiritual truth. Notice how this contrasts with the physical operation which was given to Abraham and performed with human hands.

Salvation is the operation of God upon hearts of believers. He cuts away the old life of self-effort from the repentant heart, and places the saints *in Christ*. The *law works* are the illustration; Christ is the reality. Since salvation is God's spiritual work and not physical, then no physical element or rite has any part in it.

To gain the right perspective, read again Colossians 2:9-10: "For in him dwelleth all the fulness of the Godhead bodily. And ye are complete in him." When we are in Him, there is absolutely nothing needed to finalize or seal salvation. We are *complete*!

COLOSSIANS 2:11*b*—'In putting off the body of the sins of the flesh by the circumcision of Christ."

This is God's work for the saint *in Christ*. His death on the cross cuts away the selfishness of sin. "The body of the sins of the flesh" is more correctly rendered "the lump of self." It is not speaking of the physical body but of the "mass" or "lump" of the old nature, self. As one might say, "This is the body of the class," meaning the group, the assembly; so the "body of the flesh" refers to the sinful nature and not to physical flesh. Remember, this has nothing to do with physical things. This is heart circumcision, a reality and not a rite, removal of sin and

not removal of flesh. The operation of God is not on part of the body, but the transformation of the whole person. "If any man be in Christ, he is a new creature: old things are passed away; behold, all things are become new" (2 Co 5:17). This is conversion, regeneration, sanctification, salvation!

God wants to make us spiritually whole, and we must submit to the great Physician as our Surgeon and Saviour before we are *complete in Christ.* You and I have many unfinished projects because we ran out of time or money or interest. But this is not true with the Lord! He is the Author and Finisher of our faith, and He continues to complete us day by day as we grow in grace. When a baby is born, the mother's first question is, "Is he all right? Is he perfect?" A babe in Christ (a new convert) can be complete even though he is still young spiritually; he is the temple of the Almighty. His capacity might be small, but he begins to grow.

A new baby may be complete at birth with two hands and feet and one head, but he begins to grow and becomes more complete. No, he does not grow any more heads, but he should become wiser! "Beloved, now are we the sons of God, and it doth not yet appear what we shall be: but we know that when he shall appear, we shall be like him; for we shall see him as he is" (1 Jn 3:2).

Baptism

COLOSSIANS 2:12—"Buried with him in baptism, wherein also ye are risen with him through the faith of the operation of God, who hath raised him from the dead."

Just as circumcision is used as a picture of salvation, so now baptism is another illustration of God's spiritual work. This verse does not refer to the rite of water baptism. Physical elements have no part in spiritual things; there is no need of water baptism to complete or help our righteousness, for we are counted complete *in Christ* by faith. Water baptism does not put us into Christ.

Water baptism is performed by human hands, but the baptism here spoken of is "through the faith of the operation of God." The One who raised Christ from the dead is the One who raises believers from spiritual death and places them *in Christ*. This is spiritual baptism, the baptism of the Holy Spirit. "For by one Spirit are we all baptized into one body [the church of Christ]" (1 Co 12:13a).

The word *baptize* is the English form of the Greek word which means "immerse into, identify with, dip under and bring up out of." It is used in connection with the believers' union with Christ and being immersed into His church, His body. It has nothing to do with water in this context.

The immersion into Christ can never be performed by clergy, or be sponsored by proxies, for no one can have faith for another. "None of them can by any means redeem his brother, nor give to God a ransom for him" (Ps 49:7). Each must come for himself.

Rituals or rites of any church cannot help to save or safeguard salvation. "Not by works of righteousness which we have done, but according to his mercy he saved us" (Titus 3:5).

Note that the word *baptism* is used in the New Testament in several ways. We are told that the children of Israel were "baptized unto Moses in the cloud and in the sea" (1 Co 10:2). This had nothing at all to do with either spiritual or water baptism, for they were not all saved persons, and neither did they go through the water of the Red Sea. It was dry ground! This passage simply means that they were all identified with Moses in the same experiences.

Then John the Baptist baptized in the river Jordan, but this was only for the Jews, to prepare for their coming Messiah whom they expected would immediately set up His kingdom. When He did not, they crucified Him. This was not spiritual baptism or salvation.

Jesus was baptized to picture His death, burial and resurrection (only immersion could picture this), and He was baptized to give an example for all believers to "fulfil all righteousness" (Mt 3:15). He also spoke of His "baptism into death" on the cross (Lk 12:50). This was His alone.

Then there is the important baptism of the Holy Spirit. This is salvation. "If any man have not the Spirit of Christ, he is none of his" (Ro 8:9b). This takes place at the moment of receiving Christ (Eph 1:13), and this is what is being portrayed in Colossians 2:12.

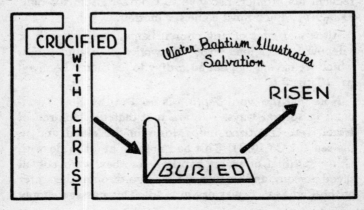

Finally, there is believer's baptism, which is a picture of salvation. The public testimony of water baptism is to follow conversion because God commands, "Believe and be baptized." It is not a means of salvation but a picture of death to the old sinful life, burial with Christ, and resurrection to live a new life *in Christ*. It is not a picture of the washing away of sins. (This subject is covered further in the author's book *God's Will Made Clear*.)

Water baptism is commanded for all who are identified with Christ and are *in Him*, and for them alone. This is not *law works* but *love works*. To be baptized with water before being saved is *dead works*.

Therefore, all believers are reckoned by God to be dead to Satan's family, buried with Christ, and risen to new life (spiritual life), and all this is the operation of God and not by our own works.

Salvation

COLOSSIANS 2:13a—"And you, being dead in your sins and the uncircumcision of your flesh."

The Gentiles were outcasts from the earthly nation of Israel, and were considered "dogs" by the self-righteous Jews. Before they were saved, they were also outcasts from God and were dead in sin (even as all unbelievers are God-rejectors, and therefore God-rejected). They needed the Saviour.

COLOSSIANS 2:13b—"Hath he quickened together with him, having forgiven you all trespasses."

To *quicken* is to "make alive," to raise from the dead. This is another picture of salvation. This does not say that we are made alive by baptism or circumcision or works, but that we become alive *with Him!* This was God's doing when He forgave us all trespasses. "And you hath he quickened, who were dead in trespasses and sins" (Eph 2:1). Those who are *in Christ* have spiritual life, and only these can know God's way is easy.

NEW MAN

MASS OF SELF

GOD'S WORK

Release from self

Removal of sin

Re-creation

Regeneration

COLOSSIANS 2:13*b*—"Having forgiven you all trespasses."

Forgiveness is for those who can confess sin (not for infants who do not have sin to confess even if they could), and no one can confess for another. With forgiveness comes new life. "Know ye not, that so many of us as were baptized into Jesus Christ were baptized into his death? Therefore we are buried with him by baptism into death: that like as Christ was raised up from the dead by the glory of the Father, even so we also should walk in newness of life" (Ro 6:3-4). This again is the picture of what takes place when one is saved by the operation of God when He forgives our sin. From then on we are *in Christ*.

This is the message of the book of Colossians. God is willing to amputate the old sinful way of life and make us alive *in Him*. We all need spiritual surgery! Conversion!

A mother who was intensely antagonistic against the gospel came to a meeting just to please her daughter. Afterward we had a chance to chat together; and she admitted, "I was one of those you talked about tonight who turn their backs on God!"

After a longer conversation about the way of salvation, that night she prayed and asked Christ to be her Saviour. She had a long way to go as far as a new way of living was concerned, but she knew she had been born spiritually and was *in Christ*. From then on she began to change though, and discarded one by one the things of her old sinful life. She gave her testimony to her friends with whom she used to play cards and drink. The reactions were varied. Some made fun of her and called her a fanatic. Others were polite and aloof, and still others were tolerant and told her to come and see them again when she had gotten over her religious "kick."

But as the weeks rolled by, they could see something had really happened to her; though they could not understand it, yet they did appreciate the fact that her enthusiasm did not wane.

I stood with her as we poured the last bottle of whiskey down the drain. I will never forget that day.

Forgiven, dead with Christ, buried with Him, risen with Him, and complete in Him! Glory to God!

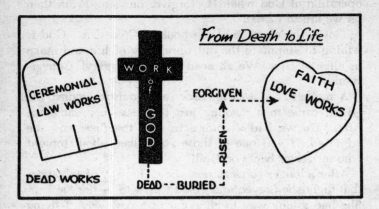

"Knowing that a man is not justified by the works of the law [religious rites and deeds], but by the faith of Jesus Christ [faith in Him, and His faithfulness to keep], even we have believed in Jesus Christ, that we might be justified by the faith of Christ, and not by the works of the law: for by the works of the law shall no flesh be justified" (Gal 2:16).

God's way is easy for those who are justified.

QUESTIONS

1. To whom was the Sabbath given? (Ex 31:12-18)
2. To whom was circumcision given? (Gen 17:9-14)
3. Who is the High Priest today? (Heb 4:14-16)
4. Is the "flesh" the selfish nature, or physical flesh? (Ro 8:5-9)
5. Is salvation spiritual baptism? (Eph 4:4-6)
6. Should water baptism be practiced in this age? (Mk 16:16; Mt 28:19; Ac 16:31-34)

7. Do infants belong to God? (Mt 18:10; Heb 1:14)
8. What does it mean to be made alive? (1 Jn 5:12-13)
9. Who is the Author and Finisher of our faith? (Heb 12:2)
10. Who are "dead in sin"? (Eph 2:11-12)

8

PROVISION BY CHRIST

Sins Nailed to the Cross (Col 2:14-17)

OVER MY DESK at home is a large photo of my husband, and when he is out of town I find myself talking to it sometimes! Yes, it's silly, I know, but I love him! However, when he is home I do not sit and talk to his picture; it is only a shadow of him!

The Bible is full of pictures too. Beginning when sin was born in the human race, God gave a picture of the coming Saviour who would give His blood as the covering for sin, when the blood was shed to provide a covering of animal skins for Adam and Eve. Of course animal blood could never remove sin, but it was an illustration, or shadow, of the atonement through Jesus Christ.

Sin Debt

COLOSSIANS 2:14a—"Blotting out the handwriting of ordinances that was against us, which was contrary to us."

The entire human race has sold out to the devil in spiritual bankruptcy, and we have nothing to pay except an eternity in the lake of fire. "It is appointed unto men once to die, and after this the judgment" (Heb 9:27). We all need the Saviour! A sinner is a debtor.

Some are *out* and *out* in sin and sold completely to the devil; others are *down* and *out* in the very dregs of sin; still others are *up* and *out*, for they are self-righteous and think they need no Saviour; and then, some are *in* and *out*—in churches, but out of Christ! But all are *all out, way out!*

One look at the holiness of God should cause us to drop to our knees in shame, crying, "Woe is me!"

The handwriting that is against us is the debt of sin that serves to convict us before God. It is contrary to us, and we are contrary to it. But what are the ordinances that are against us? This refers to any and all disobedience against God, and especially the one unpardonable sin of rejecting the message of the Spirit in presenting the Saviour (Jn 16:8-9). One lie makes one a liar, one theft makes a thief, one murder makes a murderer. "Every mouth may be stopped, and all the world may become guilty before God" (Ro 3:19*b*). Sin is disobedience to God in any form at all. It is not just breaking certain laws (as the Ten Commandments), but rebellion against the known will of God given for Christians in the New Testament (1 Jn 3:23).

Reform will not remove the blot, for no debtor dares to tell his creditors, "Just forget the debt and I'll do better in the future!" A debt gives the creditor power over the debtor. In fact, in olden days the debtor was literally unsafe until the debt was paid, for the creditor actually threatened to skin him alive! There is where the term "take it out of your hide" originated.

Sin Blotted Out

COLOSSIANS 2:14—"Blotting out the handwriting . . . took it out of the way, nailing it to his cross."

God says, "I have blotted out, as a thick cloud, thy transgressions, and, as a cloud, thy sins: return unto me; for I have redeemed thee" (Is 44:22). The same truth is given in the New Testament. "Repent ye therefore, and be converted, that your sins may be blotted out" (Ac 3:19). All the failure of keeping the law of Moses was taken away from the Old Testament godly by the death of Christ on the cross, even as all the sin of the New Testament saints is also nailed to His cross. He paid our debt. The nails that pierced His hands and feet and fastened Him to the cross were nailed there by God because of your sin and mine. This is His way of saying, "Paid in full!" He took our *sin debt* out of the way, and

GOD'S WORK OF GRACE

turned our *law debt* to a *love debt* that will take all eternity to pay.

Perhaps you remember how country stores used to keep a spindle on the counter, and when a bill was paid it was stuck on that nail. The perforation of the nail hole meant it was paid in full. There was a custom in ancient China of nailing paid bills to the doorpost outside the house. It was a proud day when all the bills were nailed there! God nailed the sins of the believer to the cross.

This payment of the death penalty is the only way to balance the books with God. One obedience can never atone for one sin any more than a million good deeds could blot out one sin. Therefore only the nail-scarred Son of God could wipe the slate clean. Praise His name!

Satan Defeated

COLOSSIANS 2:15a—"And having spoiled principalities and powers."

Here again mention is made of Satan's kingdom of darkness which Christ stripped of victory at His resurrection. How the devil tried to keep Him from being the Saviour! He instigated Herod to kill all the babies when Jesus was born; He tempted Jesus to get Him to forfeit His rights as God; he stirred up men to try to kill Him before the right time to die; and he even tried to make Christ shrink from God's will in the garden of Gethsemane. He tried hard enough, but to no avail. When Christ rose from the dead, thus proving that He is God, Satan lost everything.

In the garden of Eden God promised that the devil would bruise the Saviour's heel (Gen 3:15), and this he did when Jesus died, but the prophecy also said that the Saviour would bruise the enemy's head, and this was done when Christ rose from the dead. Satan is a potentially defeated foe but, like the snake that he is, he will not admit that his hopes are crushed, so he is working overtime.

COLOSSIANS 2:15b—"He made a shew of them openly, triumphing over them in it."

Calvary is God's way of showing what He thinks of sin, and the resurrection is His way of showing what He thinks of Jesus Christ. He made a public triumph over all forces of evil and stripped the devil of his power over the souls of the saints so that there is no need for them to be defeated in sin. "Greater is he that is in you [the Spirit of Christ], than he that is in the world [Satan]" (1 Jn 4:46).

All this was done openly. Christ's death and resurrection were for all to see. They were done openly in that they clearly fulfilled all types and prophecies.

Just as conquerors in olden times chained their prisoners to the chariot and made them run alongside in public humiliation, so Christ has doomed the devil to the lake of fire where he will be in the lowest department. He certainly will not be the king of hell!

The cross was a triumph. The shout of "It is finished!" was the cry of victory. "O death, where is thy sting? O grave, where is thy victory? But thanks be to God, which giveth us the victory through our Lord Jesus Christ" (1 Co 15:55, 57).

Not only has the devil received a knockout blow, but even death has lost its sting. The saints *in Christ* do not die; they merely shuck off the sick old body and keep right on living with the Lord. This is liberation! There is no need for any "last rites," for they already have the "rights" to their Father's home. Christ paid the last rites on the cross!

Signs and Types Ended

COLOSSIANS 2:16—"Let no man therefore judge you in meat, or in drink, or in respect of an holyday, or of the new moon, or of the sabbath days."

Here the Christians are instructed that they should not need anyone to set them straight on these matters, for they should know that the old system of Mosaic worship is now ended in Christ. All the Jewish feasts and feast days were but shadows of the person and work of the Saviour until He came, and now He had come so the shadows were empty.

The Jews had seven yearly feast Sabbaths as well as the weekly sixth-day Sabbath of rest. However, absolutely none of these has been carried over and given to the church. "Meat" and "drink" in this context refer to Jewish religious customs and not to harmful or habit-forming things.

This is the answer to two more errors that lashed against the church at Colosse, namely, that salvation is gained by keeping laws and rituals, and that the Old Testament laws are for Christians. But such fallacies are anything but out of date, for the same errors permeate many denominations today, and a great proportion of Christendom in our age still believes that ordinances, such as baptism and the Lord's Supper, will aid in absolving sin, and that the physical things and priesthood of the Old Testament are also for Christians. For those who are not saints *in Christ* to be baptized or to take communion only brings upon them greater damnation. "The sacrifice [religious deed] of the wicked is an abomination to the LORD" (Pr 15:8a).

Sunday Observance

The saint *in Christ* is not under obligation to keep the Jewish feast Sabbaths or their day of rest. But, on the other hand, if those under the shadow of truth who did not have the indwelling Holy Spirit, as believers do today, were commanded to keep one day a week as special unto the Lord, then shall we do less? The saints in this age keep the Lord's Day, the first day of the week, as a day of worship. The Sabbath was not changed; it just was not given to the church.

Why keep Sunday? Sunday is the first day of the week and it was on this day that Christ rose from the dead, the most important remembrance for the saints *in Christ*. Also, Christ met with His disciples twice for the breaking of bread after His resurrection on the first day of the week. Then, the Holy Spirit came to earth to indwell believers on the first day of the week, Pentecost. The disciples met on the first day of the week for preaching and communion; and offerings for the Lord's work are to be gathered on the first day of the week. With the example of Christ, of the Spirit and the apostles, this makes the Lord's Day the Christian day of worship.

My missionary mother always made Sunday a special day for us. Even though we children went to Chinese church services (which we did not exactly enjoy!), yet we always had a special Sunday dinner and a walk through the hills with father.

God's instructions regarding the Old Testament Sabbath might well be applied to our day of worship, for it certainly embodies the principle of worship. "Turn away thy foot from the sabbath [step around it, count it special], from doing thy pleasure on my holy day; and call the sabbath a delight, the holy of the LORD, honourable; and shalt honour him, not doing thine own ways nor finding thine own pleasure, nor speaking thine own words: then shalt thou delight thyself in the LORD" (Is 58:13-14). If this is what He expected from His ancient saints, should we then care less for a day of worship?

"Let us hold fast the profession of our faith [our testimony] without wavering; (for he is faithful that promised;) and let us consider one another to provoke [stir up] unto love and to good works; not forsaking the assembling of ourselves together, as the manner of some is; but exhorting one another [by preaching]; and so much the more, as ye see the day approaching" (Heb 10:23-25). The Lord's return is even closer now than when those words were penned, so we should not need to be judged on this matter. We should know!

Shadows

COLOSSIANS 2:17—"Which are a shadow of things to come; but the body is of Christ."

When there is a shadow, there is also reality. The Old Testament mode of Jewish worship was a picture of the Son of God who would be the "Lamb of God, which taketh away the sin of the world" (Jn 1:29). Before He came, godly men waited by faith. "But when the fulness of the time was come, God sent forth his Son, made of a

woman, made under the law, to redeem" (Gal 4:4-5).
Christ is the reality, "the body is of Christ." He came
to fulfill the law and the prophets and the sacrifices and
feasts, so now all types and pictures of Judaism have
been completed and done away. He is the One who
cast the shadow of the cross over the Old Testament, and
now the same shadow lies across all New Testament truth
as well. Christ is the reality!

A shadow means there is a Reality

A shadow is empty when Reality comes

It is in this shadow of the reality, Christ, that we live
as willing slaves to please Him who paid our debt of sin
on the cross of Calvary. In Bible days a bondslave who
had been set free by a kindly master might offer to serve
for the rest of his life. In such a case his ear would be
pierced by an awl as he stood beside the doorpost, and
the piercing was a sign that he was serving willingly, for
love. Christ was pierced on the cross for us. So should
we not be willing to live our life for Him?

The Chinese New Year is a very important holiday.

No one can collect any debts on that day! Creditors who have been on the prowl after debtors have to give up on that day. Debtors come out of hiding and stroll down the main streets in their holiday gowns, smiling and bowing to their creditors as they say, "Happy New Year! Happy New Year!" The next day they go back into hiding again!

However, for all who have received Christ as personal Saviour, there is no need to hide from God. Our debts are paid, and so every day is a happy one. Glory to His name!

"Therefore if any man be in Christ, he is a new creature: old things are passed away; behold, all things are become new. And all things are of God" (2 Co 5:17-18).

God's way is made easy for those who are His!

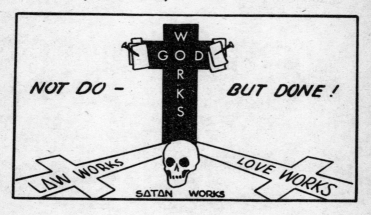

QUESTIONS

1. What is sin? (Ro 5:19; Jn 16:9)
2. How do we know Christ was nailed to the cross? (Jn 19:18)
3. Who are Satan's emissaries? (2 Co 11:13-14)
4. Does the Bible teach that the devil has a low place in hell? (Is 14:12-15)
5. Do Christians die spiritually? (Jn 11:25-26)
6. What do "meat" and "drink" mean in connection with religion? (Heb 9:10)
7. What are the other Sabbaths for the Jews? (Lev 23)
8. When are offerings to be brought for the Lord's work? (1 Cc 16:2)
9. When did the early Christians meet for preaching? (Ac 20:7)
10. What was one of the proofs that Christ is God? (Jn 10:17-18)

9

PAGANISM VERSUS CHRIST

Truth and Errors (Col 2:18-23)

HUMAN INTELLIGENCE is sometimes a handicap when it comes to spiritual things that must be taken by faith. And yet, God's Word is the answer even for the scholar and educator.

A gentleman with a keen scientific mind came to our Bible classes recently and drank in the doctrines of God like a thirsty soul. He often spoke of how much he was learning and how glad he was that he had received the Saviour. However, he still had some doubts that troubled him.

Realizing that he was an honest seeker, I suggested that he and his wife stay and talk after the next class. They did. We discussed many subjects at length, and I will always remember the look of relief and peace as each question was answered. After they went home, he told his wife that he was now completely cleared of doubts that had threatened his peace of mind. I was glad that we had that talk, for it was early the next morning that God called him home to glory.

Now he is face to face with his Lord, and he knows

fully the answers to everything in the whole universe!
Human intellectualism no longer hinders.

Paganism of Voluntary Humility

COLOSSIANS 2:18a—"Let no man beguile you of your reward
in a voluntary humility."

God's work must be done in God's way. Therefore,
religious principles and practice must be in harmony with
His Word, or else, no matter how zealous or faithful or
sincere, they count for less than nothing with Him.

The reward spoken of here stands for God's approval
and blessing both now and in eternity. All this is for-
feited when error creeps in to rob the saints of their
fidelity to the truth, or when they are working under
the flag of a wrong religion or liberal and modernistic
church.

What is the first error set forth here? Voluntary humility! This is actually pride of self-imposed humility, if

you can imagine such a paradox! This corresponds with what we know today as self-penance and taking delight in self-affliction for suffering's sake in the hope of gaining acceptance with God. This artificial humility led to the idea that "we are so very humble, so we need mediators to represent us before God." This begets many errors, including spiritualism.

Paganism of Mysticism

COLOSSIANS 2:18b—"Worshipping of angels."

The Colossian pagans believed that between God and man were many orders of angelic beings that demanded obedience and worship. But the Bible says that there is one God and only one Mediator between God and men, the God-Man, Christ Jesus, who gave Himself as a ransom (1 Ti 2:5-6). There was danger of the new Christians in Colosse being caught up in this mysticism, thinking they would show humilty because they dared not come directly to God in prayer. This is idolatry as well as error.

So why do some even in our day neglect the Bible and develop a whole system of prayers to saints in heaven, calling upon angels and the apostles, and considering Mary as mediatrix? The Bible is very up to date, and sin is very old-fashioned!

COLOSSIANS 2:18c—"Intruding into those things which he hath not seen."

This savors of the occult, dabbling into spiritualism, which is really demonism. Remember, God does not communicate with any who are not washed in the blood of the Lamb and in harmony with His Word (and neither do the angels or the saints in heaven), so spiritualism is really contact with demons. Such are an abomination to the Lord and their destiny is the lake of fire (Rev 21:8; Deu 18:9-13).

The correct rendering of this phrase is "Intruding into those things which he hath seen." However, even though it is left in the first rendering, "Intruding into things which he hath not seen," the idea is the same. This includes emphasis on trances, visions and mystical experiences which are wrongly attributed to God's working. Some might be due to sheer overactive imagination, and others to actual demon manifestations, but whatever the case, they are not of God.

In this church age there is no longer need for signs and revelations from God, for now we have the New Testament which is the very last word of truth. Furthermore, there is severe warning against any so-called new message

from the Lord: "Ye shall not add unto the word which I command you, neither shall ye diminish ought from it, that ye may keep the commandments of the LORD your God" (Deu 4:2). The apostle John, the last inspired writer of Scripture, closes his revelation with the warning, "If any man shall add unto these things, God shall add unto him the plagues that are written in this book" (Rev 22:18b).

On the day of Pentecost, when the Holy Spirit came to indwell the believers, He gave certain signs to prove He had really come. Since spirit is not visible, audible or tangible, God gave certain miracle manifestations to assure the saints that they were indeed indwelt by the Spirit, and to vindicate the authority of the apostles so that the world might know they were the ministers of God (Heb 2:3-4). These signs were three: the *sound* of a rushing mighty wind, the *sight* of tongues of fire, and the *ability* to speak in languages they had not learned (Ac 2:1-12).

Signs and miracles were for the believers in the early church days when there was no New Testament to give forth God's Word, and when it was needful to prove to the Jewish Christians that Gentiles were also to be included in the church.

The gift of tongues carried three requirements: those who received the gift spoke in a known language they had not learned, they knew what they were saying, and they were understood by those who heard. After all, language is for the sole purpose of communicating with people. God knows the thoughts, so there is no need to use the tongue to speak to Him; neither is there need to invent some so-called "ecstatic language" (babblings) for Him. God knows English!

God does no unnecessary miracles. If there were need for the gift of tongues today, it surely would be given to the dedicated missionaries who have to sweat through language school!

Adherents of the popular trend toward seeking the "gift of tongues" in our time, state that only those who have spoken in ecstatic language have the Holy Spirit. Nothing could be farther from the truth. Every believer is indwelt by the Spirit at the moment of salvation (Ro 8:9) and is sealed with the Spirit (Eph 1:13). Jesus did not speak with tongues, and neither did D. L. Moody or Hudson Taylor! Why do men water down the Word of God, twisting and misinterpreting it without comparing scripture with scripture?

A Christian was challenged as to whether she had been given a new tongue since she accepted Christ as her Saviour. She replied, "Yes, He gave me a new tongue all right. I don't swear anymore!" That is the new tongue God gives to believers today!

Those who drift into the error of the "tongues movement" usually hold some other wrong doctrine, or they are not well taught in the Word. They are seeking a feeling of acceptance with God, or a boost over spiritual depression, or some tool for success in service, and they do not understand that all we need for life and godliness is already ours *in Christ*. We do not get more of Him, but He wants more of us!

When asked what his speaking in ecstatic sounds did

for him, a man replied, "I'm speaking the language of the Spirit! I don't know what I'm saying, but God does!"

I reminded him that the Spirit prays in the heart of the saints with "groanings [yearnings] which *cannot be uttered*" (Ro 8:26). He does not make audible sounds!

After all, it is possible to produce utterances by self-hypnotism. If we do not know what we are praying, then God is not interested! He speaks to the mind in tune with, and filled with, the Word, and not to an empty mind. But the devil looks for a FOR RENT sign, and then he moves in gladly!

Some claim that their incomprehensible utterances are "angel tongues." But, just what language do angels speak? In Bible times angels who communicated with men spoke the language of men. To speak with the tongues of angels (1 Co 13:1) refers simply to the graciousness and authority by which angels spoke to men.

Even the devil can work miracles, so Christians must watch for his traps which are set for those who do not "rightly handle the word of truth." He is quite willing that men have religion just as long as it is not the truth. It is not spiritual to be superstitious.

COLOSSIANS 2:18d—"Vainly puffed up by his fleshly mind."

Seeking for extrasensory experiences and pseudohumility is actually a form of pride. "Vainly puffed up" is emptiness and soap bubbles! What an indictment! This is self-conceit in attainment of some mystical ability (which is intellect apart from God), thinking that acceptance with God comes from attaining some status.

Instead, the Bible tells us that we only have access to Him by faith in Christ.

Christianity

COLOSSIANS 2:19a—"Holding the Head."

This is the core of Christianity. Since He is the Head of all creation (1:15-17), the Head of angels (2:10, 15), the Head of the church (1:18), and is actually God Himself (1:19; 2:9), therefore the only way to acceptance with God is to be in connection with Him.

The core of error is not holding Christ as the Head. To try to come some other way is indeed to be "on strike against the management!"

COLOSSIANS 2:19b—"From which all the body by joints and bands having nourishment ministered."

When Christ is the Head, His Spirit binds all saints together. "In whom all the building fitly framed together groweth unto an holy temple in the Lord: in whom ye also are builded together for an habitation of God through the Spirit" (Eph 2:21-22). All supply of life and strength comes from the Head through His Spirit.

COLOSSIANS 2:19c—"And knit together, increaseth with the increase of God."

The body of Christ, the church, is knit together in love (2:2) by the Spirit, who also provides the nourishment of the Word to keep the body growing and healthy and with strength to serve. He does give endowment of power for victory over sin and for witnessing, but He does no unnecessary miracles.

So, the body of Christ is made up of the saints of God who are banded together by the Spirit of God, with the nourishment of the Word of God, and knit together in the love of God, and they increase with the increase of God! What need, then, for other mediators or signs or mysticism? Paul's ministry was to "open their eyes, and to turn them from darkness to light, and from the power of Satan unto God, that they may receive forgiveness of sins, and inheritance among them which are sanctified by faith" (Ac 26:18).

COLOSSIANS 2:20a—"Wherefore if ye be dead with Christ from the rudiments of the world."

Since Christ is the Head, then nothing else counts with the believer except to please Him. Any religious laws and practices that are not Christ-centered and Christ-directed have no value. To be "dead with Christ" is to be finished with the old life of sin and error (materialism

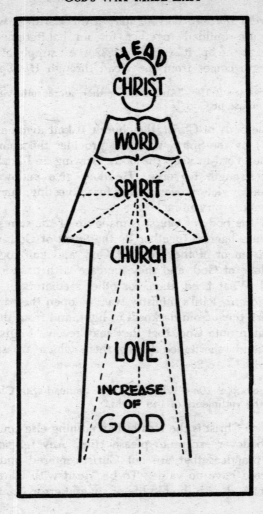

in worship), and to begin a new life as a member of His body. Death is the separator. Dead to Satan's dictates and doctrines and alive unto God to be doubly privileged to live for Him who is our Head.

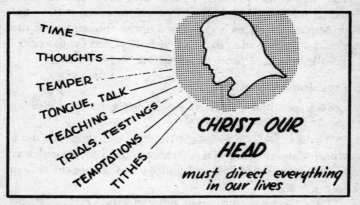

TIME

THOUGHTS

TEMPER

TONGUE, TALK

TEACHING

TRIALS. TESTINGS

TEMPTATIONS

TITHES

CHRIST OUR HEAD

must direct everything in our lives

1. Our *time* is His, so are we good stewards?
2. Our *thoughts* are His, so what do we cherish and think about?
3. Our *temper* is His, so does He control it?
4. Our *tongue* is His, so is it truthful and wholesome?
5. Our *teaching* is His, so is it biblically sound?
6. Our *trials* are His, so do we trust Him in them?
7. Our *temptations* are His, so do we allow Him to give victory over them? He is concerned for all that concerns us.
8. Our *tithes* are His, so does He control our pocketbook?

The rudiments of the world are man-made superstitions and prescriptions involved with physical elements as a practice of religion which are not after Christ (2:8) and have not been given in the New Testament for our age. This would include old Judaism and its temporary rites which have not been given to Christians, as well as the principles, practices and persons under the control of the world system under Satan, which is called "the world." To all these the saints *in Christ* are to be dead.

Paganism of Ritualism

COLOSSIANS 2:20b—"Why, as though living in the world, are ye subject to ordinances."

"Ordinances" are ordained things. A lot depends upon who ordained them. Those who are dead to the old way of living are no longer to be subject to the world system in religion.

True, God gave ordained things in the Old Testament worship (priests, robes, lamps, altars, etc.) which were types of Christ. All these have now been fulfilled by His coming, and done away. They have never been given to Christians.

Then there were ordained things invented by the Pharisees and imposed upon the Jews which were never given by God at all. This intricate system of traditions was denounced by Jesus: "Making the word of God of none effect through your tradition, which ye have delivered" (Mk 7:13).

And now in our times there are also man-stipulated rituals which have never been ordained by God. Only two ordinances have been given by God for all believers in the church age, and these are the Lord's Supper (communion) and baptism. Neither are aids to salvation, and both are only for those who are *in Christ*. As someone might look at a timetable for a Sunday train but read the column marked "For Weekdays Only," so men try to follow laws clearly marked "For Israel Only" when they are not under the old dispensation of law, or "For Christians Only" when they have not yet received Christ as their personal Saviour. Wrong teaching lays aside the commands of God, but Christians are to lay aside the commands of men!

GOD'S TIMETABLE

OLD TESTAMENT — for Jews ....
Religious rites, Laws of Moses

NEW TESTAMENT — for believers .....
Christian commands, Ordinances

Be sure to look at the right schedule!

COLOSSIANS 2:21-22—"(Touch not; taste not; handle not; which are all to perish with the using;) after the commandments and doctrines of men?"

One thing is certain: this is not speaking of harmful or habit-forming things. The things referred to here are taboos concerning religion which were not given to Christians by God.

What a sad list of man-legislated practices often bog down churches in our times, where observing rules and sacraments and religious days take the place of simple trust in Christ! How it must break the heart of God! "Now the Spirit speaketh expressly, that in the latter times some shall depart from the faith, giving heed to seducing spirits, and doctrines of devils; speaking lies in hypocrisy; having their conscience seared with a hot iron" (1 Ti 4:1-2).

"Things" such as relics, beads, holy water, images, candles, and keeping Lent, which began during the time when the Bible was a closed book, have been attached to the message of the gospel, until justification by faith has almost been lost. These *law works* and *dead works* and *heathen works* keep men from God. "By the works of the law shall no flesh be justified" (Gal 2:16b). Christianity is not attained by what men do, but by what Christ has done! All physical things are to perish with time and fade away. Spiritual things remain forever. Man is so earthbound that he becomes entangled with material gadgets in his efforts to earn salvation, and he does not hold Christ as the Head.

Paganism of Will-Worship

COLOSSIANS 2:23a—"Which things have indeed a shew of wisdom in will worship, and humility."

This is a self-will mode of worship which is not really worship of God at all. With high-sounding words, the philosophy of man's wisdom might intrigue the uninformed, but it does not impress those who know God's

Word. Pretense of humility can easily be seen through by the spotlight of the Spirit of God.

COLOSSIANS 2:23b—"And neglecting of the body; not in any honour to the satisfying of the flesh."

This was the thinking of the Stoics as well as today's heathen "holy men" of India who believe they are attaining holiness by inflicting pain and deprivation upon their bodies. But the believer's body is the temple of the Holy Spirit, so it does not honor Him if we neglect or harm it. The Bible teaches the denial of sin and selfishness, and nothing more. And yet, devotees all over the world are inflicting pain on their bodies in the hope of atoning for their sins. They make pilgrimages, wear hair shirts, lie on a bed of spikes, vow never to speak again, gaze into the sun until blind, and live a life of poverty—all with the sad and mistaken idea that they are pleasing God. If only they would read His Word!

In the Philippines, Good Friday is celebrated by some

SELF-
PENANCE
on
Good Friday

who slash their backs with razor blades until the blood
gushes, and then flog themselves while they prostrate
themselves along the "stations of the cross," and finally
soak their bleeding backs in the sea for further agony.
All this in the name of Christianity! How it must grieve
Him who gave Himself for our sins!

Imitating the sufferings of Christ is not His way of
salvation, for to bypass His free gift is to dishonor Him.
What hopelessness! Those who do not worship God by
His way do not worship Him at all. Christ is not their
Head. The devotee is actually saying, "Look at me! See
how holy I am—how humble I am!" This is Satan's way
of clouding the reality of the Spirit-filled life.

Voluntary humility, mysticism, ritualism and will-wor-
ship are all self-glorification and not giving honor to
Christ as the Head. They are satisfying the pride of the
flesh and impressing others who do not know the Lord.
"Having a form of godliness, but denying the power
thereof: from such turn away" (2 Ti 3:5). No wonder
God warns, "Be not carried about with divers and strange
doctrines. For it is a good thing that the heart be established with grace; not with meats, which have not profited
them that have been occupied therein" (Heb. 13:9).

How sad that so many do not know what there is to
know, and do not know that they do not know it. And,
what is worse, they do not want to know.

As saints *in Christ* we have the privilege of increasing
with the increase of God as we yield to the Spirit. "For
the perfecting of the saints, for the work of the ministry,
for the edifying of the body of Christ: till we all come
in the unity of the faith, and of the knowledge of the

Son of God, unto a perfect man . . . speaking the truth in love, may grow up unto him in all things, which is the head, even Christ" (Eph 4:12-15).

This is God's way made easy!

QUESTIONS

1. When will Christians receive rewards? (I Co 3:11-15; 2 Co 5:1-10)
2. What will rob our reward? (2 Jn 8-11)
3. What is the work of God's angels? (Ps 34:7; Heb 1:14)
4. What do idols represent to the heathen? (1 Co 10:20)
5. Why was the gift of tongues given in Acts 10:44-48?
6. What does the word *vain* mean in Scripture? (Ec 1:2-11)
7. Is the body of Christ, the church, "one"? (Ro 12:4-5; 1 Co 12:14-27; Eph 4:4)
8. Where else is Christ called the Head? (Eph 1:22; 4:15)
9. Who is "dead" with Christ? (Ro 7:4, 24; 8:13; Gal 5:24)
10. What did the Old Testament ordinances represent? (Heb 9:1-12)

10

PARTAKERS WITH CHRIST

Christ Our Life (Col 3:1-4)

No FINE CLOTHES or jewels could change a rotting corpse. It needs life! We do not believe in "zombies," which are the figment of science-fiction imagination, but God does tell us that the unsaved are "living dead" souls who have turned their backs on Him and are living in spiritual death and separation from Him, even though they are still physically alive. No amount of morality or education or religion will give them life.

Resurrection

COLOSSIANS 3:1a—"If ye then be risen with Christ, seek those
things which are above."

This is speaking of spiritual life rather than the resurrection of the body. Transport yourself to the eternal
past when God planned salvation and Christ volunteered
to give Himself for the sins of the believers, and then
grasp what this really means. When Christ died on the
cross for believers' sins, God counted that we were crucified there with Him (even though we were not yet born).
And when He rose from the dead, God counted that we
rose with Him. There must be a death before there is a
resurrection.

This is deep spiritual truth, but we believe it because
God says it. The apostle Paul also said, "I am crucified
with Christ: nevertheless I live; yet not I, but Christ
liveth in me: and the life which I now live in the flesh
I live by the faith of the Son of God [by the faithfulness
of the Son of God], who loved me, and gave himself for
me" (Gal 2:20).

Just as seed in the ground gives up its life to bear a new
plant, so salvation means death to the old life and resurrection to a new one *in Christ*. "Our Saviour Jesus Christ,
who hath abolished death [spiritual death and damna-
tion], and hath brought life and immortality to light
through the gospel" (2 Ti 1:10). This risen life means
a new mind, new affections, new ambitions, new appetites,
new habits and a new hope. It is not an easy journey,
but a safe one!

When Jesus raised Lazarus from his physical death and

he came forth from the dark tomb, imagine how glad he was to be freed from the graveclothes as well! When we are given newness of life we should long to come out of the grave of self-seeking and sin and fling off worldly ideas and habits, leaving behind wrong religion and beginning to "worship in spirit and in truth." Even as a flower bulb planted in the ground dies so that it might begin a new life, so we are *in Christ*, and as we grow that new life will be revealed.

COLOSSIANS 3:1*a*—"Seek those things which are above."

This is the outward proof that we are truly saved and risen with Christ. If our mind is set on Him, then our activity will center around Him, and we will seek to please Him and look forward to being with Him. Like the woman who lost her coin and must have made the dust fly in seeking it, so we are to clean out every catchall closet and the shelf behind the door with all the old grudges and sinful habits.

Too often, though, instead of really seeking the will of God, we are more like the man who goes to find his socks and then stands at the top of the stairs and shouts to his wife, "Where are my socks?" He does not really look for them; it's a lot easier to let her find them! But God tells us, "Seek ye first the kingdom of God, and his righteousness" (Mt 6:33). This is our life's delight. It is one thing to be a chrysalis, but it is no gain to remain one forever. It is time to break forth and soar to things above.

This does not mean that we are to be so heavenly minded that we are no earthly use, but it does mean that

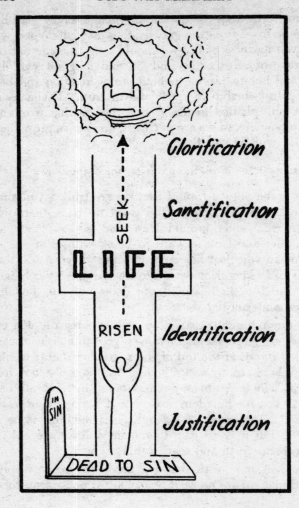

our first thought should be of our Lord, to ask His approval on what we do on earth.

COLOSSIANS 3:1*b*—"Where Christ sitteth on the right hand of God."

The fact that Christ is sitting speaks of His finished work of redemption. "After he had offered one sacrifice for sins for ever, sat down on the right hand of God" (Heb 10:12). The right hand of God is the place of authority and power and honor. This is a symbolic term, since God is Spirit and does not have a physical body or hand as such. It simply means that Christ and the Father are together. Concerning Christ, the prophet says, "The LORD at thy right hand" (Ps 110:5). So Jehovah God is also at the right hand of Christ! Two Persons, but one God!

Here is proof that Jesus does not die over and over again when the communion is celebrated. He offered one sacrifice for sins forever. "We are sanctified through the offering of the body of Jesus Christ once for all" (Heb 10:10). "So Christ was once offered to bear the sins of many" (Heb 9:28).

Consecration

COLOSSIANS 3:2a—"Set your affection on things above."

"Set" is another word for *seek*. As the growing plant strains toward the light of the sky, so the believer's whole bent of life is to seek the will of God. "Where your treasure is, there will your heart be also" (Mt 6:21). Things above are not just glory and joy and a place, but the *Person;* not just His blessings, but our *Beloved!* This changes our self-seeking into willingness to be made willing about everything God sends us.

When the heart is set upon someone, there is longing when that person is absent, and there is delight when he or she is present. We often say of a boy in love, "His heart is elsewhere!" The heart of the saint *in Christ* should be elsewhere—in heaven.

My brother Bob and his wife were medical missionaries to Ethiopia. When Italian forces invaded that small country, Bob was commissioned by the emperor to head the Red Cross. He was at the front lines, operating day and night as he cared for the wounded from the bombings. It was during that time that he received the news that their first baby had been born. He was elated with joy, for they had waited long for that child. His leave was overdue, and he wrote of his hope of soon seeing his loved ones. Yes, his heart was elsewhere all right, far from the

"HIS HEART WAS ELSEWHERE ALRIGHT !"

battle-scarred burning heat of the African desert! (Bob never did see that baby though. He was killed before he ever got to take his leave. His body lies buried in Addis Ababa, the capital of Ethiopia.)

Our citizenship is in heaven. "While we look not at the things which are seen, but at the things which are not seen: for the things which are seen are temporal; but the things which are not seen are eternal" (2 Co 4:18). This is not cloud nine, but the Lord!

When we reach glory, we will not be strangers if our heart has already been there. Even the things on earth can be sent on ahead and will be waiting there for us! No, we cannot take them with us. But when we use them for the Lord's glory, there is a crown of glory; by giving to the Lord's work, our money is laid up in heaven; by winning souls, there will be those in heaven to greet us. So send it on ahead!

The Chinese believe that the dead will need material

things in the afterlife, so they make paper replicas of furniture, horses, money and clothes, and carry them in the funeral procession to the grave. There they are all burned in a grand bonfire amid firecrackers to give a happy send-off to the departed, and frighten the evil spirits away.

But we Christians do not send make-believe things to glory. It has to be the real thing—time and strength, godliness and giving, gratitude and love—and none of these will be lost. Jesus said, "Whosoever will save his life shall lose it; but whosoever shall lose his life for my sake and the gospel's, the same shall save it" (Mk 8:35). Earthly coin is not transferable, so invest it in soul-winning projects in order that dividends will keep coming in for eternity. Gold has no value in heaven; there the streets are paved with it! God can make gold as easily as He makes dirt, so let's not set our hearts upon it (Deu 8:18)!

COLOSSIANS 3:2b—"Not on things on the earth."

DROWNED in HONEY!

THINGS ON EARTH

What are the things on the earth? There is nothing wrong with preferring riches to poverty. But when the mind is set on possessions, this is worldly and earthly and very unsatisfying. "Your riches are corrupted, and your garments are motheaten. Your gold and silver is cankered. . . . Ye have heaped treasure together" (Ja 5:2-3). This is like a bee drowning in a pot of honey.

On the other hand, "The blessing of the Lord, it maketh rich, and he addeth no sorrow with it" (Pr 10:22).

Material things are not good or bad in themselves, but it is "the love of money is the root of all evil: which while some coveted after, they have erred from the faith, and pierced themselves through with many sorrows" (1 Ti 6:10). The things on earth could all be summarized as the things of *self*, selfishness. (The suffix *ish* often has a derogatory meaning, and in slang it means "horrible"! That is exactly what "self-ish" means—horrible self!) What an empty goal this is! Earthly indulgences do not satisfy; they only whet the appetite for more and more. Popularity wanes, possessions wear out, beauty fades, health fails. Perhaps this sounds rather morbid, but it is morbid! It is time that we faced facts and set our affection on things above, for what will we have when all else fails?

Earthly things should be mere stepping-stones to the ivory palaces. Are they? Or do we hold on to them as if they would last forever?

"Love not the world, neither the things that are in the world. . . . For all that is in the world, the lust of the flesh, and the lust of the eyes, and the pride of life, is not of the Father, but is of the world. And the world passeth away, and the lust thereof: but he that doeth the will of God abideth for ever" (1 Jn 2:15-17).

Identification

COLOSSIANS 3:3—"For ye are dead, and your life is hid with Christ in God."

Before salvation, each person has in him the natural sinful nature called the "old man." This is the "mass of self" which is contrary to God. At conversion a new nature is given which is the "new man, the spiritual man, the inner man." This new self does not love sin. "Whosoever is born of God doth not commit sin; for his seed remaineth in him: and he cannot sin, because he is born of God" (1 Jn 3:9).

Those who have been risen with Christ are to count the old nature as dead, and the old life of self-effort in Satan's family as finished. This is what God regards as so, and He tells us to practice it as so: "Reckon ye also yourselves to be dead indeed unto sin, but alive unto God through Jesus Christ our Lord" (Ro 6:11).

Sin is not misfortune but the act of rebellion and self-will against God. It is wonderful that those who accept God's offer of spiritual life are made alive! "And you hath he quickened [made alive], who were dead in trespasses and sins . . . even when we were dead in sins, hath quickened us together with Christ" (Eph 2:1-5). When men sow to their flesh, they reap corruption, and corruption stinks!

But the believer is to be dead to the old pattern of externalism in religion as well as dead to the guilt and damnation of Satan's family, and dead to worldliness and

defeat and doubt. The things of sin should be as repugnant to the saint *in Christ* as a decaying corpse. Paul said, "The world is crucified unto me, and I unto the world" (Gal 6:14). Conversion was the end of Saul of Tarsus as he emerged the apostle Paul! Is this true of us? Did that old selfishly sensitive part of us come to an end at conversion and a new nature come alive? God grant it!

How much attention people give to their outer man! They spare no expense for dentist, doctor, clothes, food, hair, etc., but what about the inner man? How much time each day is spent on spiritual food and care?

"Ye are dead." A dead man has no interest in debauchery; he is dead. So the saint *in Christ* is crucified with Christ, and the old sins that nailed the Lord to the cross are as hateful and horrifying as a putrid cadaver. "Knowing this, that our old man is crucified with him [with Christ] . . . that henceforth we should not serve sin" (Ro 6:6).

This is what is meant by the believers being dead. It certainly does not imply that they are dead and dull personalities. Indeed, no! They are alive unto God! "Like as Christ was raised up from the dead by the glory of the Father, even so we also should walk in newness of life" (Ro 6:4*b*).

This new life is bound up in the same bundle, as it were, with Christ in God. This is security! This is God's doing.

PLANT YOURSELF !

Suppose you placed a flower bulb on a table beside a pot of prepared earth and said, "Now start growing bigger and bigger until you're big enough to jump into that pot!" Just how long would you have to wait? Ridiculous? Of course! It is just as foolish for a lost sinner to hope to get better and better until he is good enough to belong to God. God must plant him into the soil of faith *in Christ* before he can begin to grow at all.

Once we are alive *in Christ,* we can never be lost again unless He is lost! Since we do not earn salvation, therefore we cannot lose it. Jesus said, "I give unto them eternal life; and they shall never perish, neither shall any man pluck them out of my hand. My Father, which gave them to me, is greater than all; and no man is able to pluck them out of my Father's hand. I and my Father are one" (Jn 10:28-30). We cannot get ourselves away from the Almighty, and Satan cannot steal us away, and neither can he steal heaven away from us. He cannot rob the bank of heaven! Christ is the caretaker. When we are hid with Christ in God, then we are not going to be such eager customers when the devil dangles his baubles before our eyes.

We are hid from damnation and judgment, with Christ in God!

> God is so very near to me, nearer I cannot be;
> For in the person of His Son, I am as near as He!

Glorification

COLOSSIANS 3:4a—"When Christ, who is our life, shall appear."

Christ our life! This is the meaning of being a saint *in Christ.* He is our very center of gravity, our everything for time and eternity, the goal as well as the means to the goal and the power to reach the goal. As Paul said, "For to me to live is Christ, and to die is gain" (Phil 1:21). Only the saints *in Christ* can say "to die is gain." Heaven is gain socially, for we shall be with Him; it is gain physically, for we shall have a perfect resurrection body; it is gain materially, for we shall have all the riches of glory; it will be gain spiritually, for we shall be sinless. Hallelujah!

> Spiritual life comes *from Christ*: He is the source.
> Life is *on Christ*: He is the foundation.
> Life is *in Christ*: He is the security.
> Life is *through Christ*: He is the enablement.
> Life is *to Christ*: He is the destination.
> Life is *by Christ*: He is the Saviour.
> Life *is Christ!* We possess Him and He possesses us, and this provides security.

A bird in the ark was as safe as the elephant. It was not the strength of the animals but the ark that kept them! Neither did Noah find safety by holding on to the ark, but because he was inside and it held him.

"He that hath the Son hath life; and he that hath not the Son of God hath not life . . . that ye may know that ye have eternal life" (1 Jn 5:12-13). No wonder God's way is easy!

When He shall appear, we shall be with Him! Not maybe, but for sure! Christ will appear to us when we die, and we will be with Him in heaven; He will appear to the saints who will be raptured when He comes to catch them away; He will appear when He comes to reign, and every eye will see Him. In every instance the saved will be with Him! This is a guaranteed promise. "It is Christ that died, yea rather, that is risen again, who is even at the right hand of God, who also maketh intercession for us" (Ro 8:34).

COLOSSIANS 3:4*b*—"Then shall ye also appear with him in glory."

GLORIFICATION!

Full Bloom

The flower bulb is planted in the good soil. It dies, springs up in a new shoot and then grows into a new plant, showing above the ground. It develops buds, leaves, and then the full flower! This is the ultimate purpose of salvation: to see Him, to be like Him, and to be with Him! "And they shall see the Son of man coming in the clouds of heaven with power and great glory" (Mt 24:30*b*), and you and I will be there too! What a day that will be! Revelation day! "When he shall come to be glorified in all his saints, and to be admired in all them that believe" (2 Th 1:10). Celebrity in person!

But—and here is the one warning note—our measure of glory in that day will depend upon how faithful we are now and whether Christ is indeed our very life and center of focus on earth. If not, we shall even then suffer loss. "Abide in him; that, when he shall appear, we may have confidence, and not be ashamed before him at his coming" (1 Jn 2:28).

On the mission field we had the privilege of telling of the Saviour to lost souls who had never heard the message before, not even once. Some of those mountaineers in the Philippines had only heard the name of Christ as a swear word, and they lived in fear of evil spirits and the witch doctor. People such as this do not doze when they hear of the Saviour and His love! I can still see their eager faces and hungry eyes as they exclaimed, "Then there is hope?"

Thank God, there *is* hope! But one mountain chief listened as my husband told God's plan of salvation, and then he asked, "Is this all true?"

"Yes, it is true."

"Did your father and great-father and your great-great-father know of this?"

"Yes, they knew."

The wizened old man was silent for a moment, and then he spat his mouthful of betel-nut juice, and said, "My father never heard this and my great-father never heard this. And yet, you have only now come to tell us. It could not be true!"

"For the love of Christ constraineth us [draws us] . . . and that he died for all, that they which live should not henceforth live unto themselves, but unto him which died for them, and rose again" (2 Co 5:14-15).

Love for the Lord makes God's way easy!

QUESTIONS

1. What does being "risen with Christ" involve? (2 Co 5:15)
2. What are the things above? (Ja 1:17)
3. What does it mean to worship in spirit and truth? (Jn 4:22-26)
4. Where is Christ today? (Ac 7:55-56; Ro 8:34, Eph 1:20)
5. What does God give to those who give up things for Him? (Mt 19:29)
6. What is lust? (Ja 4:3-4)
7. When do we have life? (Jn 3:36; 4:14; 5:24, 26; Titus 1:2; 1 Jn 5:12-13)
8. Can the believer be lost again after he is saved? (Jn 17:11, 24)
9. What is eternal life? (Jn 10:10-11; 14:6)
10. What can separate the Christian from the love of God? (Ro 8:35-39)
11. What is the Christian's hope? (Tit 2:13)

11

PUT OFF AND PUT ON IN CHRIST
The Old and the New Man (Col 3:5-11)

AT THE WORLD'S FAIR there was an exhibition showing a man pumping water. From a distance he looked lifelike and real, but it was only a dummy. Yet, it was pumping water, and no motor or electrical agent was used. It was simply operated by the water flowing from the mains; so instead of the man pumping the water, the water was pumping the man!

What operates human beings? God says that the unsaved are Satan-directed: "Ye are of your father the devil, and the lusts of your father ye will do" (Jn 8:44a). The saints *in Christ* are to be Christ-directed, for they are indwelt by the Spirit of Christ; and the old self of sin is to shrivel up and become ineffective.

The Old Man

COLOSSIANS 3:5—"Mortify therefore your members which are upon the earth; fornication, uncleanness, inordinate affection, evil concupiscence, and covetousness, which is idolatry."

Can it be that God is speaking to Christians? He is! "But we never do such things!" Oh no? What about thoughts of impurity and sensual imagination? What about watching lustful movies and reading suggestive books, and looking at the pornographic pictures on the covers of magazines on the bookstands? What about singing worldly songs of lust and impurity? It is possible to indulge in immorality vicariously (through watching others). God would not warn us against such if no one was dabbling in it. "But fornication, and all uncleanness, or covetousness, let it not be once named among you, as becometh saints; neither filthiness, nor foolish talking" (Eph 5:3-4).

As becometh saints, sin is to be put to death. This is very personal, for it is speaking of the physical appetites controlled by our old *self,* and the shoe pinches!

There is nothing wrong with the human body, for God created it; but when men are in rebellion against God, this becomes the source of lust and depravity. What a black list of sensual practices are given here! "Mortify" means "to put to death." These are to be put to death. We can do nothing about earning our salvation, but plenty about how we live when we are saved.

"Inordinate affection" is unholy love. "Evil concupiscence" is impure thought and desire. "Covetousness" in this context is wanting that which is not ours to have; this is idolatry since it is rebellion against the will of God. All these are involved in immorality and abnormal sex practice.

BOTH are IDOLATORS

This is even the tendency of those today who "want wrongly" that which might be theirs rightly after marriage, and this is self-love and self-worship, which is idolatry.

Because the saints in Christ are risen with Him, therefore He can give power for victory over the core of evil which is the old man, the old self. True, this old nature will not be removed until we reach heaven, but that does not mean that it needs to run us. Victory is available, and this is now our part in cooperating with God by putting such sins to death.

COLOSSIANS 3:6—"For which things' sake the wrath of God cometh on the children of disobedience."

The godless world has fallen into debauchery because it does not heed the Word of God. "For this cause God gave them up unto vile affections. . . . And even as they did not like to retain God in their knowledge, God gave them over to a reprobate mind, to do those things which are not convenient [befitting]" (Ro 1:26-28).

One sin banished Lucifer from heaven, and one sin separated Adam from God and drove him from the garden; and only one sin makes you and me sinners. Shall we then expect to stand before the holiness of God with all our thousands of sins? We need the Saviour!

It was for such perversion as here listed that God brought the flood in Noah's time, and fire and brimstone upon Sodom. But today, audacious sinners flaunt righteousness.

Judgment will come! "Because sentence against an evil work is not executed speedily, therefore the heart of the sons of men is fully set in them to do evil" (Ec 8:11).

"The children of disobedience" are not small children; they are children of the devil who have chosen to disobey God. "Wherein in time past ye walked according to the course of this world, according to the prince of the power of the air, the spirit that now worketh in the children of disobedience: among whom we all had our conversation in times past in the lusts of our flesh" (Eph 2:2-3).

Wrath of God will fall upon all who resist His will, and America will not escape either! "After thy hardness and impenitent heart treasurest up unto thyself wrath against the day of wrath and revelation of the righteous judgment of God" (Ro 2:5).

The matter of immorality is very relevant today, for the issue is very much alive as men veer off the path of God's standards into irregularity of "free love" to the destruction of themselves and all that is holy. Immorality is stimulated by the fantasy life of reading materials and pictures which feed the old sinful nature, and the bent of thought is "Do what comes naturally!"

COLOSSIANS 3:7—"In the which ye also walked some time, when ye lived in them."

Before they were saved, the Colossian Christians, just like everyone else, were spiritually color blind and needed God's color chart. A color-blind driver who cannot tell

SATAN, THE MASTER.

the difference between red and green is due for a crack-up! Satan flatters the sinner by saying, "You're as good as anyone else. Everyone's doing it. It's not considered shocking anymore. Enjoy yourself!" But he fails to say that "the way of the transgressor is hard!" He is a master hypnotist!

However, some might challenge this statement and say, "I've never been immoral, and I live a clean upstanding life. So I don't fit into this picture!"

Before God, *any* disobedience is sin, and sin is idolatry. The greatest sin of all is not to receive the Saviour. So this is the walk of one who is not a saint *in Christ!*

Put Off the Old Man

COLOSSIANS 3:8—"But now ye also put off all these; anger, wrath, malice, blasphemy, filthy communication out of your mouth."

Does this come closer to home? Sins of disposition and speech! The sins of the old man are to be avoided like the plague, for all is to be Christ-centered instead of self-centered when we are born from above. The Christian is to execute what God has already sentenced, and put to death the old practices and put off the domination of the old man. "Let not sin therefore reign in your mortal body, that ye should obey it in the lusts thereof" (Ro 6:12). In the Lord's power, and day by day as we yield to Christ, victory is available. This is the expulsive power of a new affection. When we love the Lord, we hate sin!

However, the core of sin is not always easy to define since we have lived so long in it, and we do not always recognize just what is *self* and sin. God tells us to search out our motives and practices and dig up the clods of years of self-will. "Break up your fallow ground: for it is time to seek the LORD, till he come and rain righteousness upon you" (Ho 10:12). Hard, unplowed, caked soil of the sinful mind, set in its own way, needs to be broken up, with the stones of rebellion removed and the thorns of self-will pulled up. Then, and only then, is it time to plant!

This is God's work in the willing heart. We certainly cannot do this alone. Our part is to claim His presence and power and cooperate in being willing.

The mountaineers in the Philippines do not bother to dig up the fallow ground when they plant. They simply fell the larger trees and set fire to the whole area. As flames roar up the mountainside, they leave the ground littered with stones and charred rubble; but the men make holes in the earth with a sharp stick and drop in a kernel of corn. That is all! As time goes by, they go out to find

MOUNTAIN PLANTING

the harvest amid the tangled debris and jungle under-growth.

But this is not God's way of planting. Conviction, con-trition and conversion form no primrose path, especially if it is the old *self* that is being dug up!

These verses are warnings against the sins of lust, which are idolatry; the sins of covetousness, which are idolatry; the sins of temper, which are idolatry; the sins of the tongue, which are idolatry. None give God His place as Head.

Anger is hot temper; wrath is temper boiling over; malice is anger turned to ice.

Blasphemy involves self-opinion expressed in words in opposition to God. When man says, "I want—I think—I will—" and challenges the character and wisdom of God, this is blasphemy.

Filthy communication, of course, includes unclean words, untrue words, unkind words, and wrong doctrine as well. "Out of the abundance of the heart the mouth speaketh" (Mt 12:34b).

For example, a man was amazed to hear that a rider in his car pool was a Christian. "Why," he exclaimed, "he tells the dirtiest stories of them all!"

Suppose you carefully collected seeds from your prize flowers and planted them in a prepared plot. What a shock it would be if you had a harvest of thistles instead! Neither can a child of God bring forth a life of constant disobedience to Him and obedience to the devil. "Let no corrupt communication proceed out of your mouth, but that which is good to the use of edifying, that it may min-ister grace unto the hearers" (Eph 4:29).

COLOSSIANS 3:9—"Lie not one to another, seeing ye have put off the old man with his deeds."

This is the reason for righteousness. The new life *in Christ* cannot bring forth "sin bias." Lying includes untruth, part truth, exaggeration, and false teachings contrary to the Bible. It also includes acting a lie, hypocrisy and sham. We cannot fool God.

Put On the New Man

COLOSSIANS 3:10—"And have put on the new man, which is renewed in knowledge after the image of him that created him."

There must be a putting off before there can be a putting on. The prodigal son probably needed a bath, and his pigpen rags burned, before he put on the best robe! Cleansing before clothing! Here now is something every saint can print on a picket: "Down with the old man!" We pass from the death cell to new life!

Now we come to the positive side of the challenge. This is re-creation and renewal; not whitewashed, but washed white; not just a clean shirt, but a clean man! Anything less is a subnormal Christian life because "no man can serve two masters." Just trying to serve *one* is full-time work, but to serve two is enough to give a nervous breakdown! Perhaps this is why some Christians do break down.

No faith is justifying unless it is sanctifying, so the saint is given a spiritual garment for his spiritual walk. Have you noticed how the Bible connects clothing with righteousness, and nakedness with depravity? The believer is clothed with Christ's righteousness. "My soul shall be joyful in my God; for he hath clothed me with the garments of salvation, he hath covered me with the robe of righteousness" (Is 61:10).

The new man is renewed in knowledge (is constantly being renewed), and this knowledge is the wisdom and knowledge that comes from knowing the Lord and knowing His will and obeying His Word, for regeneration is a new mind. "And be not conformed to this world; but be ye transformed by the renewing of your mind, that ye may prove what is that good, and acceptable, and perfect, will of God" (Ro 12:2). The will of God is good because He is good; it is good for us and will make us good. It is acceptable since it comes from God, and we are to accept it gladly as our own will. The Bible is the one place to find the will of God.

The word *costume* comes from the custom of wearing certain distinguishing clothing such as police uniforms and spacemen's suits. Just as costumes are noticeable, so conversion and conduct should be noticeable. Not religious robes! This is speaking of the costume of our character, and the habit of the heart.

As a little girl in boarding school in China, I always knew when the seasons changed because on that certain date we all changed into different clothes. Sometimes we shivered and sometimes we melted, but there was a change made, and it showed!

One who is renewed after the image of the One who created her, is not going to mold herself into the pattern of Hollywood or the godless world, but she will be willing to be modest and feminine. The man who is renewed after the image of Christ is not going to indulge in the practices of sin, but he will be masculine and a gentleman.

Some businessmen say, "I can't give to missions; my money is all tied up!" How much better if they would say, "My money is all tied up in missions; I can't afford to spend it on tobacco or the theater!"

A godly life is the best way to say thank you to God.

One Man in Christ

COLOSSIANS 3:11—"Where there is neither Greek [Gentile] nor Jew, circumcision nor uncircumcision [ritual or no ritual], Barbarian, Scythian [uneducated or educated], bond or free [employee or employer]: but Christ is all, and in all."

In Christ all are one. There is no difference spiritually; there is the same standard of godliness. There is no different code of ethics for the housewife or the businessman, for the pastor or his people, for the native or the missionary. Social differences, yes! Spiritual differences, no! In this day of seeking equality, the one great equality that men overlook is equality of godliness.

When the climate of the heart is renewed *in Christ,*

the life should bloom into the ultimate goal: Christ is all and in all.

Have you ever tried to grow African violets? A friend had trouble with her sickly plants no matter what she tried. Then one day she happened to place them in a different window. Presto! They began to bloom and kept right on blooming!

Is Christ all and in all to us? Does He approve all we do and everywhere we go? Is He a welcomed Guest at our parties and social outings? If not, there is some sin somewhere.

Victory is available. Then why do we so often not see it? It is not that God has not given, but that we have not taken; we really do not want it. That old nature needs knocking out over and over again, and this we can do through the power of God if we desire victory.

Are we disobeying some known command of God? Have we failed to dig up the fallow ground of the past

and clear the slate? Are we not spending time in prayer and Bible study and communion with the Lord? Are we not attending a sound Bible-believing church? Then, no wonder there is no victory!

"Neither yield ye your members as instruments of unrighteousness unto sin: but yield yourselves unto God, as those that are alive from the dead, and your members as instruments of righteousness unto God . . . now yield your members servants to righteousness unto holiness" (Ro 6:13, 19*b*).

God's way is easy when we are willing for His way!

QUESTIONS

1. Who are Satan-directed? (Jn 8:44; Ac 26:18; 2 Co 4:4; 1 Jn 3:8; 5:19)
2. What does God think of immorality? (Eph 5:3-5)
3. What is to be "mortified"? (Ro 8:13)
4. On whom does the wrath of God come? (Ro 1:18)
5. Who are the "children of disobedience"? (Ro 1:24, 28; Eph 5:6)
6. What was the state of all saints before they were saved? (1 Co 6:9-11)
7. What is to be put off and what is to be put on? (Gal 5:19-21; Eph 4:22-32; Titus 3:3)
8. What is the destination of unrepentant liars? (Rev 21:8, 27)
9. What counts with God? (Gal 6:15)
10. Should all saints be "one"? (Gal 3:28; Phil 1:27)

12

PURITY IN CHRIST

Robe of the Bride (Col 3:12-14)

AT A WEDDING the flowers and decorations are all secondary to the breathless expectancy to see the bride. As she starts down the aisle there is the excited whisper, "There she is! Isn't she lovely!" The next day the papers will describe her gown and veil, and she will cut out the article and keep it with her bridal portrait!

There is a contrast though between this wedding and the spiritual relationship of Christ and His bride, the church. On glory day it will be the Bridegroom whom the world will acclaim, and the bride will be included only because she is His bride. "When Christ, who is our life, shall appear, then shall ye also appear with him in glory" (Col 3:4). On that day Christ will come to earth to set up His kingdom, and the church will come with Him. "God also hath highly exalted him, and given him a name which is above every name: that at the name of Jesus every knee should bow, of things in heaven, and things in earth, and things under the earth: and that every tongue should confess that Jesus Christ is Lord, to the glory of God the Father" (Phil 2:9-11).

187

The Robe

COLOSSIANS 3:12a—"Put on therefore, as the elect of God. . . ."

In the meantime, it is well to note the robe of godliness which the bride, the saints, is to put on and to wear here on earth.

All believers *in Christ* have been given the robe of Christ's righteousness when they are saved. "And to her [the bride] was granted that she should be arrayed in fine linen, clean and white: for the fine linen is the righteousness of saints" (Rev 19:8). This, God's gift to all who are saved, is the righteousness of Christ Himself.

But the robe we are considering now is the Christian life and character. For the sake of illustration, suppose we represent the special life of Christians—that which shows that they are the bride—as the special garment worn by a bride to show that she is a bride. Because the believer has put off the old man and put on the new, and

Christ is all and in all, therefore practical righteousness is to be the pattern of life, the wedding robe.

The Headpiece for the Robe

COLOSSIANS 3:12*b*—"The elect of God."

The first part of this character costume is that we are the elect of God, chosen *in Christ*. We will represent this as the crowning demonstration of God's grace, the tiara or headpiece of orange blossoms. The bride is chosen to be saved. "According as he hath chosen us in him before the foundation of the world, that we should be holy and without blame before him in love: having predestinated us" (Eph 1:4-5). Christ is now choosing His bride in this age of grace. "Them who are the called according to his purpose. For whom he did foreknow, he also did predestinate . . . them he also called" (Ro 8:28*b*-30). "Elect according to the foreknowledge of God the Father" (1 Pe 1:2*a*).

But this is also a two-way love match, for the saints have the privilege and responsibility of choosing Him. The bride is made up of all the blood-washed throng (the church universal, and someday triumphant) that He has gone to prepare a place for in heaven. He said, "I go to prepare a place for you. And if I go and prepare a place for you, I will come again, and receive you unto myself; that where I am, there ye may be also" (Jn 14:2*b*-3). He is also preparing us for the place!

Before the world began, God loved His own; He knew who would make up the bride, and these are "the elect." How amazing that His love is focused upon each individual, even as it is upon the entire group of saints; just as if the whole Amazon River flowed only to water one lone daisy! How this should make us rejoice! So cheer up, ye saints of God!

"According to the power of God; who hath saved us, and called us with an holy calling, not according to our works, but according to his own purpose and grace, which was given us in Christ Jesus before the world began" (2 Ti 1:8b-9).

The Bodice of the Robe

COLOSSIANS 3:12c—"Holy and beloved."

To be holy means to be set apart for God—sanctified for Him and for no one else. As a betrothed girl is set apart for her beloved and should throw away the telephone numbers of her old boyfriends, so the believers are promised and set apart for the Bridegroom. This is *positional holiness.* We do not wait until the actual day of the marriage supper of the Lamb in heaven to be set apart for Christ. We are set apart the moment we accept His proposal to become His beloved.

Since holiness involves the heart, suppose we represent this as the bodice of the gown of Christian character. Positional holiness soon overflows from the heart into *practical holiness* as we forsake all others and love, honor and obey our Bridegroom as long as life shall last.

Being raised on the mission field and in boarding school, I had very little interest in domestic things. My youthful ambition was to be a tennis champion! When I was first married I had to learn to cook and keep house, and my poor husband was the guinea pig! He was very patient because he loved me, but I offered him many a burnt offering! I did my best though, for I loved him!

As the psalmist says, "With my whole heart have I sought thee: O let me not wander from thy commandments. Thy word have I hid in mine heart, that I might not sin against thee" (Ps 119:10-11). The more we love our Lord, the less we will love ourselves. After all, when we are all bound up in ourselves, we are a mighty small bundle!

The Veil of the Robe

COLOSSIANS 3:12c—"Holy and beloved."

"Beloved" is the special name for the saints *in Christ*, and His love covers us like a bridal veil covers the bride. So we will picture this love as the veil for the robe of Christian character.

"Behold, what manner of love the Father hath bestowed upon us. Herein is love, not that we loved God, but that he loved us" (1 Jn 3:1a; 4:10a).

We have nothing that merits His love, but the miracle is that God places His own value upon us and then loves us for the value He Himself has given us! Amazing! He says, "I have loved thee with an everlasting love: therefore with lovingkindness have I drawn thee" (Jer 31:3b).

The Skirt of the Robe

COLOSSIANS 3:12c—"Bowels of mercies, kindness, humbleness of mind, meekness, longsuffering."

Now we come to the skirt of the robe of Christian character for the bride of Christ. This involves a long train of godly qualities which God will work in us if we are willing to say, "Not my will, but thine be done!" To share our heart with worldliness will mean that we will soon find ourselves wholehearted for the world and fainthearted for the Lord.

Mercy is love softened by sympathy. Only those who have suffered and been lonely can truly give sympathy to those who suffer or are lonely. "The God of all comfort; who comforteth us in all our tribulation, that we may be able to comfort them which are in any trouble, by the comfort wherewith we ourselves are comforted of God" (2 Co 1:3b-4). "Bowels of mercies" is an ancient term meaning a heart of mercy. After all, even the word *heart* does not mean the physical organ that pumps blood through our veins! These are terms referring to the real *you*.

"Kindness" comes from a Dutch word *kind* which means "child," and this stands for family love for one's own child. Now of course this verse is not speaking only of human affection for our children, but rather the care and consideration for all who are in the family of God, the saints. This should be the same concern and courtesy that a loving parent gives to his own bairn.

How this would take care of jealousy and faultfinding and bickering among Christians! It isn't normal to be beloved and holy and not be kind.

This is where we bump up against the giant *self*, the enemy of graciousness. It is sometimes so easy to show sunshine and smiles to casual acquaintances, but to be irritable and rude at home. These things should not be so! It would be better to try some of the sweetness and light on the family! They might faint, but it would be good for them and for you! Kindness is concerned with the happiness of others.

"Humbleness of mind" is esteem for others instead of for self, and this should be genuine humility and not pretense—an honest attitude toward God and others. Boasting of success in Christian work is not humbleness of mind. "Humble yourself in the sight of the Lord, and he shall lift you up" (Ja 4:10). This must be in the sight of God, remember, so there can be no fraud.

Some attempt false humility by saying, "If I can only get to heaven, I'll be willing to take a back seat!" But God says we are to labor for an "abundant entrance" and not a back seat. He wants us as close to Himself as possible.

True humility yields to the Lord completely, gives every ounce of strength to obey Him, and does not take the credit for any success. "For we preach not ourselves, but Christ Jesus the Lord. . . . But we have this treasure in earthen vessels [our human frame], that the excellency of the power may be of God, and not of us" (2 Co 4:5-7).

"Meekness" is another addition to the skirt of the gown of Christian character. This is not weakness but submission to the will of God and ability to give in to others on nonimportant matters. Moses was said to be a meek man, but he certainly was not weak. Can you see him carrying those tablets of stone down the mountain and then crashing them to the ground in righteous anger! Jesus was said to be meek as a lamb before its shearers, yet He was not weak. What strength of character it took to face angry mobs, still the tempest and raise Himself from the dead.

"Longsuffering" is another characteristic of the robe. This means to suffer long *in Christ*, and be loving and lovely at the same time. Long-suffering gives a soft answer, renders good for evil, and suffers in self-control. How often we judge others by ourselves, and we do not like them because they are too much like ourselves! There needs to be graciousness among those who are saved by grace.

COLOSSIANS 3:13a—"Forbearing one another, and forgiving one another, if any man have a quarrel against any."

"Forbearing" is to hold back everything unkind—retaliation, revenge, sharp retorts. "Forgiveness" means to hold nothing back of love and good will. This goes both ways: holding back temper and not holding back love. After all, in the light of eternity, are personal grudges so important that we hold on to them even to the detriment

FORBEAR HOLD BACK!

LOVE · FORGIVE · HOLD NOTHING BACK!

Don't throw that stone!

of others? After an eternity in glory, what comfort will there be to look back and think, *Well, anyway, I was right about that quarrel with my mother-in-law two million years ago!*

COLOSSIANS 3:13*b*—"Even as Christ forgave you, so also do ye."

This is the New Testament basis of forgiveness. Thank God, He does not forgive us according to how we forgive others! Instead, we are to forgive because we are forgiven. "And be ye kind one to another, tenderhearted, forgiving one another, even as God for Christ's sake hath forgiven you" (Eph 4:32). As the Bridegroom, so the bride.

All quarrels begin with self. Then what happens? Self gets hurt, and then there is self-pity!

"Forgive" really means "put it forth from you," banish, dismiss and forget it! A Christian lady felt convicted because she had not spoken to her relative for many years after a quarrel. She asked how to make the move for reconciliation. I suggested that she send a pretty card with a pleasant greeting for Easter. She did, and received a card in return. Result? They had a meeting and wept in confession and reunion.

The Belt of the Robe

COLOSSIANS 3:14—"And above all these things put on charity, which is the bond of perfectness."

Unfortunately the word "charity" has become very watered down until today it is used to mean mere benevolences or handouts to the poor. But the Scripture meaning is "the love of God is shed abroad in our hearts by the Holy Ghost which is given unto us" (Ro 5:5b). This is the band, or belt, that ties the robe of Christian character together and makes forgiveness and long-suffering possible. This "bond" is above all things. Little else counts if we do not love the Lord and love others.

The love of Christ "shed abroad in our hearts" for others "suffereth long, and is kind; . . . envieth not . . . is not puffed up. Doth not behave itself unseemly [is courteous], seeketh not her own [does not grasp at personal rights], is not easily provoked, thinketh no evil; rejoiceth not in iniquity, but rejoiceth in the truth; beareth all things, believeth all things, hopeth all things, endureth all things" (1 Co 13:4-7). The love of Christ "shed abroad in our hearts" for others "never faileth" (1 Co 13:8). Real benevolence is to love the gospel, live the gospel and tell the gospel.

"The bond of perfectness" is completeness. "Even as Christ also loved the church, and gave himself for it; that he might sanctify and cleanse it with the washing of water by the word, that he might present it to himself a glorious church, not having spot, or wrinkle, or any such thing; but that it should be holy and without blemish" (Eph 5:25-27).

As Christians, we are the bride of Christ! What a privilege and what a responsibility! God wants us to wear this robe in spiritual health.

"The king's daughter is all glorious within: her clothing is of wrought gold. She shall be brought unto the king in raiment of needlework" (Ps 45:13-14a). This is the "hope chest" of the King's daughter who is to be the bride of the King's Son! Unless we are a child of the King we are not eligible to be the bride of the King. Every thought and deed and word of ours for the glory of God is like a stitch in the needlework of our hope chest, the "blessed hope" chest! Not a "hopeless" chest!

This chapter might sound like a message only for women, but it is not! There is no respect of persons with God when it comes to spiritual truth; there is neither male nor female.

Are we all looking for the coming of our Bridegroom? "And the Lord direct your hearts into the love of God, and into the patient waiting for Christ" (2 Th 3:5). He is also looking for our coming to be with Him.

The Robe Rejected

Jesus told a parable about a wedding robe in Matthew 22:1-14. The king was making a feast for his son (representing God the Father preparing for His Son), but the invited guests refused to come (Israel rejected the Son). So the king invited all the people (whosoever will, Jew or Gentile) from the highways and byways, until there were many guests at the wedding. To each was

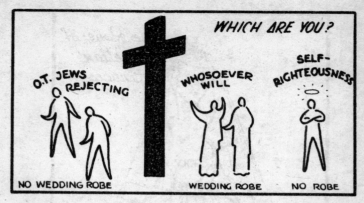

given a wedding garment. This was the local custom in Bible days, but in the parable this represents the robe of righteousness for all who accept God's invitation for salvation.

"And when the king came in to see the guests, he saw there a man which had not on a wedding garment" (Mt 22:11). Here was one who came in his own self-righteousness and did not accept God's salvation. "And he saith unto him, Friend, how camest thou in hither not having a wedding garment? And he was speechless" (v. 12). There was no excuse, for the robe had been provided.

"Then said the king to the servants, Bind him hand and foot, and take him away, and cast him into outer darkness; there shall be weeping and gnashing of teeth" (v. 13).

Now remember, a parable is pointing to some specific truth, and does not necessarily lend itself to fit every doctrinal point. The main point of this parable is very

The Robe of Christian Graces

ELECT

HOLY

LOVE

MERCY

KINDNESS

HUMILITY　MEEKNESS

LONGSUFFERING　FORBEARING

FORGIVING ALL GRUDGES

plain: some reject God's invitation entirely, some accept, and some try to gain salvation by a wrong way.

God's way is to accept Christ as Saviour and receive the gift of His righteousness, the robe of salvation, the white robe of the saints. For these, God's way is easy!

Then follows the privilege of wearing the robe of Christian character which is only for the bride, for those who have accepted the robe of His righteousness.

It is for us to determine whether we will accept or reject this wedding gown for the bride. "For he is Lord of lords, and King of kings: and they that are with him are called, and chosen, and faithful" (Rev 17:14).

QUESTIONS

1. Who are "elect"? (Jn 15:16, 19; 1 Th 1:4; 2 Th 2:13; 2 Ti 2:4; 1 Pe 2:4, 9)
2. Is Christ preparing His bride? (Eph 5:26-27)
3. Who are "beloved"? (Ro 5:8; 1 Jn 3:2; 4:11)
4. What is mercy? (Lk 6:36; Ro 12:8)
5. Why be long-suffering? (Eph 4:2; Gal 5:22)
6. Why forgive? (Lk 17:3; 23:34)
7. What is "charity"? (1 Jn 3:23; 4:12, 20-21)
8. What is the destiny of the "bride"? (Rev 21:2, 9; 22:17)
9. What is the robe God gives the saints? (Is 22:21)
10. What is the robe of self-righteousness? (Is 64:6)

13

PRACTICE IN CHRIST
Right and Wrong (Col 3:15-17, 23-24)

"GOD IS GOING to have to show me that this habit is wrong. No one is going to tell me what to do!" said a rebellious Christian who was greatly under conviction.

The answer was obvious. "Are you expecting God to send an angel from heaven just to take this harmful thing away from you? I suggest that you read the books of Corinthians, Ephesians and Colossians and see that God has already told us what is right or wrong for a Christian."

He took the suggestion and God did show him, and he obeyed the Word. It was as clear as that. This is our *practice in Christ*.

The Peace of God

COLOSSIANS 3:15a—"And let the peace of God rule in your hearts."

When God's peace is ruling, He is ruling; this takes care of confusion and conflict. There can be only one Ruler if there is to be no restlessness of the flesh against the Spirit, and no friction between conscience and ac-

tions, and no discontent between wants and supply. There will be harmony with God.

The peace of God is a matter of character rather than environment, a great calm regardless of circumstances. "The Lord is at hand. Be careful for nothing [Do not be full of care]; but in every thing by prayer and supplication with thanksgiving let your requests be made known unto God. And the peace of God, which passeth all understanding, shall keep your hearts and minds through Christ Jesus. The God of peace shall be with you" (Phil 4:5-7, 9). Only when we have peace with God who made peace for us, can we rest in the peace of God. Worry is a kill-joy. We are to be prayerful and not careful (full of anxiety). Worry reflects doubt upon God and makes us miserable and others miserable as well. By complaining and grumbling we are saying, "I don't think God knows His business! He made a mistake!" Can the unsaved thirst for Christ when they see defeated and unhappy Christians?

Anxiety comes from something we have done, or something we want and do not have, or something we imagine and fear. Bring it all to the Lord, who is "at hand," in "supplication," which means "prayer on prayer." "Thou wilt keep him in perfect peace, whose mind is stayed on thee" (Is 26:3). This means "whose imaginations stop at Thee"! This is good advice! When the peace of God is ruling, then the will of God is ruling, and this is the secret of what is right or wrong for a Christian. This gives quietness of heart.   .

COLOSSIANS 3:15b—"To which also ye are called in one body."

It was to give peace that God called us to salvation. So since we are in His church (His body, His bride), can we not now trust Him with our aches and pains and disappointments and problems? Remember, disappointments are all His appointments, so put Him between you and your circumstances. "The LORD thy God turned the curse into a blessing unto thee, because the LORD thy God loved thee" (Deu 23:5). Let not *self* be the barred door between us and God's good gifts of peace and joy.

COLOSSIANS 3:15c—"And be ye thankful."

What more normal sequence could follow the peace of God than thanks and praise? In fact, when we really trust the Almighty, thanks will even precede answers to prayer. "Now the Lord of peace himself give you peace always by all means" (2 Th 3:16). Ruffled waters can-

A PEACEFUL HEART CAN REFLECT

not reflect the mountain peaks, and neither can a troubled heart reflect Christ.

Thanksgiving will offset worry. "Although the fig tree shall not blossom, neither shall fruit be in the vines; the labour of the olive shall fail, and the fields shall yield no meat; the flock shall be cut off from the fold, and there shall be no herd in the stalls. . . ." This is a dire condition indeed! "Yet I will rejoice in the LORD, I will joy in the God of my salvation" (Hab 3:17-18).

In times of deepest despair, when my heart could do nothing but cry to the Lord, I have been caught up short by His command, "In every thing give thanks: for this is the will of God in Christ Jesus concerning you" (1 Th 5:18). Turning from begging and agonizing, I have started to praise and thank Him for *who He is* and that He loves me. What a difference this makes!

The Word of God

COLOSSIANS 3:16a—"Let the word of Christ dwell in you richly in all wisdom."

Once again we come back to those words "the word . . . wisdom." The Word of Christ is the Word of God (for He is God), and He is the Author as well as the subject matter. Therefore, if our whole being is saturated with it, and our actions are governed by it, this brings peace. "Richly" means an abundance; we will have that much godly wisdom for our *practice in Christ*.

Apart from God, men rationalize and excuse themselves in stifling their conscience by keeping away from the Word. There is a saying, "What you don't know won't hurt you!" But, what we do not know of the Word of God will not bless and will definitely hurt!

A young couple dropped out of Bible classes suddenly and completely. What happened? They explained, "We decided to stay away from Bible teaching so we wouldn't feel so guilty. Everything we read seems to hit us!" How sad! They knew enough to be responsible, so they were as miserable staying away as they had been in attending.

Satan sends out his strongest agents against the saint who wants to spend time in reading the Bible and prayer. If the Word of God dwells in us richly, we will have the answer for our own life as well as for others; there will be an ocean of blessing instead of a scant trickle. God commended those who "searched the scriptures daily, whether those things were so. Therefore many of them believed" (Ac 17:11-12).

The Bible is God's love letter, and a love letter is precious. I look forward to letters from my husband when he is away on a preaching tour, and when they come I feel glad just by looking at the envelope because I know the letter will begin with the word *Darling*.

The attention we give to the Bible shows what we think of the Writer. "And these words . . . shall be in thine heart: and thou shalt teach them diligently unto thy children, and shalt talk of them when thou sittest in thine house, and when thou walkest by the way, and when thou liest down, and when thou risest up. And thou shalt write them upon the posts of thy house" (Deu 6:6-7, 9).

This will show what is right or wrong concerning daily living.

The Hymns of God

COLOSSIANS 3:16b—"Teaching and admonishing one another in psalms and hymns and spiritual songs."

Here again God gives the two sides of witnessing: "teaching and admonishing." Teaching plants the truth within, and admonishing digs the error out!

Music is another means of teaching. However, it must be real music and not just sensual beat and psychedelic sounds! Spiritual songs are music composed by spiritual writers and sung by spiritual singers to praise and honor the Lord. "Spiritual" does not refer to so-called "spirituals" and religious folk songs, which are neither based on biblical doctrine nor consist of sounds that glorify God!

To take the weird sounds of modern worldly songs and combine them with the beat of the tom-tom, and then to incorporate this into gospel songs—just to appeal to worldly appetites—is certainly not "teaching and admonishing with spiritual hymns."

When we Christians buy recordings, we should be sure that they are sung and played by consecrated talent. Only those dedicated to the Lord can glorify Him.

COLOSSIANS 3:16c—"Singing with grace in your hearts to the Lord."

"To sing with grace" means to have love and gratitude to the Lord and to be right in our heart with Him. No amount of hymn-singing will cover up sins. To sing with grace in the heart implies worship rather than a desire to show off or to make money. Even though one might not be able to sing with the voice, it is the heart that God sees, and this is what counts with Him.

Music can rout the devil. I know, for I have often used my accordion and song to quiet a hostile throng on the mission field so that they would listen to the preaching of the gospel.

Song from sincere hearts has even helped in disastrous circumstances. For example, members of a gospel quartet, on their way across the ocean for meetings, found themselves adrift in the dark waters after their ship struck a rock in a fog. It was each passenger for himself as they clung to pieces of wreckage in the darkness and none could see the others. Then one of the singers started to sing. His wife and the other members of the quartet heard him and joined in and paddled toward him, singing, "Rock of Ages, cleft for me, let me hide myself in Thee." Soon others began to sing until the waves echoed with the hymn.

Then, suddenly out of the fogbank loomed a rescue vessel! All were taken aboard. "Your singing helped us find you," the sailors said. "We'd never have found you in the fog otherwise!"

Christians really do have a song. Singing unto the Lord shows what is right or wrong in music.

The Name of God

COLOSSIANS 3:17a—"And whatsoever ye do in word or deed, do all in the name of the Lord Jesus."

This makes the test as to what is right or wrong for a child of God very clear. "Whether therefore ye eat, or drink, or whatsoever ye do, do all to the glory of God" (1 Co 10:31). To do all to the glory of God means that we act with His approval and to show Him forth to others. Remember, the "name of the Lord" stands for His person, character and will. "Thou shalt call his name JESUS: for he shall save his people from their sins" (Mt

1:21). This does not say that He saves us *in* our sins, but *from* our sins.

In the first century the saints were given a name of scorn—Christians! But today we carry it in glad joy; we are called by His name! This certainly should tell us what is right and wrong. We don't need to wait for God to send an angel to tell us His will; it is right here as clear as black and white!

We are called by His name! How well I remember the day we arrived home after our liberation from concentration camps and entered the house my father had built and my mother had furnished. They had both gone to heaven just before our deliverance. Weak from months of starvation, and feeling broken-hearted, I thought to myself, *I'll never be a missionary again. It doesn't pay! We've lost everything—health, possessions and our parents!*

But that evening as I held my mother's Bible in my

MY MOTHER'S BIBLE

hands and turned the well-worn pages, I noticed that she had marked several passages with my name. These were verses she had dated and claimed for me just a few days before she went to glory. Here is one of the passages: "Bring my sons from far, and my daughters from the ends of the earth; even every one that is called by my name: for I have created him for my glory, I have formed him; yea, I have made him" (Is 43:6-7). The Lord spoke to me through Mother's Bible that day. I was called by His name and created for His glory; I was a Christian! There was one answer I could give to that. With tears I prayed, "Lord, I'll go again where you want me to go and be what you want me to be!" A year later we were back on the mission field again. Since then I have never forgotten that I am called by His name.

If we are honest seekers for the will of God, the following should be helpful:

DECISION ON THE DOUBTFUL

1. Is it a weight or hindrance, even though quite neutral in itself? (Heb 12:1-2)
2. Is it enslaving and habit-forming? (1 Co 6:12)
3. Is it harmful to the body which is the temple of God? (1 Co 10:19-20)
4. Does it glorify God and would He approve? (1 Co 10:31)
5. Does it detract from our love for the Lord? (1 Jn 2:15-17)
6. Is there a question mark around it? Is it doubtful? (Ro 14:5, 22)

7. Is it a stumbling block for other Christians? (Ro 15:1-2)

8. Is it a stumbling block for the unsaved? (I Co 10:22-33)

9. Does it have the appearance of evil? (1 Th 5:22)

10. Is it done as unto the Lord? (2 Co 5:15)

God does not command Christians to deny normal appetites which He has given for health and life, but rather to pivot them all around Jesus Christ. This is denial of selfishness.

"Love not the world. . . . For all that is in the world, the lust of the flesh, and the lust of the eyes, and the pride of life, is not of the Father, but is of the world. And the world passeth away, and the lust thereof" (1 Jn 2:15-17). When the world burns up, those who live only for the world will be left grasping hot, dusty ashes. These are all dying things.

"The lust of the flesh" eagerly seeks sensations which eventually turn to discontent. The "flesh" is the animal nature which is shared by brute beasts; it must be kept in control by reason.

"The lust of the eyes" is ungodly, inordinate desire stirred by the powerful "eye gate" to the mind.

"The pride of life" is another weapon of the devil. This was his own weakness, and he uses it with skill to make men sell out everything for acclaim and earthly honor. Women have sold out virtue for their name in lights; yet, how soon they are forgotten. Where will they spend eternity?

COLOSSIANS 3:17*b*—"Giving thanks to God and the Father by him."

This is now the third time we are told to give thanks, so it must be important. However, can we honestly thank God for that which does not honor Him? Of course not!

Before drinking that alcoholic beverage, thank God for it and ask Him to make you a good testimony because you drink it! You honestly cannot do so! So do not drink it!

A Christian lady told me that she kept a bottle of wine in their home because her husband liked an occasional drink. But she added, "We keep the cabinet locked, for we wouldn't want our grandchildren to find it!" But God sees inside that cabinet!

Before watching that impure movie, the production of the filthy imagination of Hollywood, pray and ask the Lord if He would enjoy it with you. Would He? If not, it is sin.

Before you buy that swimsuit, pray and thank God for the money He has given you for your needs, and ask Him if He would approve the style you are selecting. That will take care of the question of modesty.

Before you join that musical ensemble, ask God to show you if you will sacrifice your testimony by playing in it, and if the music will please Him. How sad it is to see saints *in Christ* take back the keys to their lives they once gave over to the Lord, saying, "I'd like my keys back, please. I never intended to go all the way in complete consecration!"

The Service of God

COLOSSIANS 3:23—"And whatsoever ye do, do it heartily, as to the Lord, and not unto men."

Here again is the phrase "whatsoever ye do." If God would approve, do it heartily; if not, don't do it at all!

Some challenge by saying, "Oh now, there's nothing in the Bible about smoking!" Yes there is! The Bible says, "Whatsoever ye do," and smoking is something you do! So any Christian who wants to use the filthy weed that smells up the house, burns holes in the furniture, scatters ashes on the carpet, stains the teeth and fingers, reeks on the breath, and leads children to follow the example to slow suicide and lung cancer, and squanders the Lord's money to pay for it—he must "do it heartily, as to the Lord!" God forbid!

COLOSSIANS 3:24—"Knowing that of the Lord ye shall receive the reward of the inheritance: for ye serve the Lord Christ."

Any saint *in Christ* who is not serving the Lord is serving the devil. There is no halfway house here! The unsaved person lives in sin and loves it; the consecrated saint may lapse into sin, but he loathes it. However, one backslider can do more harm than twenty Christians can do good.

"Let not then your good be evil spoken of: for the kingdom of God is not meat and drink; but righteousness, and peace, and joy in the Holy Ghost" (Ro 14:16-17). Listen to this verse: "Now the God of peace . . . make you perfect in every good work to do his will, working in you that which is wellpleasing in his sight, through Jesus Christ; to whom be glory for ever and ever. Amen" (Heb 13:20-21).

How amazing it is that God gives the gift of salvation, the power to serve Him, and victory over sin, and then He crowns it all by giving a reward for what we do for Him! What grace!

But, remember, rewards are for service and only for sanctified service. Paul said, "I have fought a good fight, I have finished my course, I have kept the faith: henceforth is laid up for me a crown of righteousness" (2 Ti 4:7-8). There is no crown without a fight! Saints will enter into rest from their labors, but too many are not laboring much, and they certainly have not been fighting against sin very much! "Rest in the Lord" does not mean that we should be worldly parasites!

COLOSSIANS 3:25—"But he that doeth wrong shall receive for the wrong which he hath done: and there is no respect of persons."

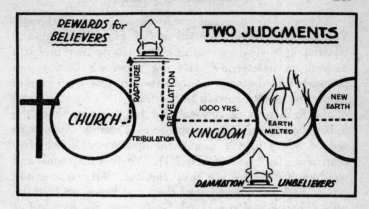

Divine justice will chasten as well as reward. Since this is addressed to the saints *in Christ*, Paul is not speaking now of the last great white throne judgment for condemned souls. Thank God, no believer will ever stand before that judgment of damnation! "There is therefore now no condemnation [damnation] to them which are in Christ Jesus" (Ro 8:1).

However, every saved person will come before the Lord in glory to give account of how he has lived as a Christian. This is called the judgment seat of Christ for the believers' works. "For we shall all stand before the judgment seat of Christ. . . . So then every one of us shall give account of himself to God" (Ro 14:10*b*, 12). It is at this judgment in heaven that God will say to us, "Well done!" or we shall suffer loss. "Every man's work shall be made manifest. . . . If a man's work abide . . . he shall receive a reward. If any man's work shall be burned, he shall suffer loss" (1 Co 3:13-15).

All reward or loss is not just for future judgment though. There is blessing of the Lord now if we are faithful, and chastening if we are unfaithful, because we reap on earth as well as in eternity. "Be not deceived; God is not mocked: for whatsoever a man soweth, that shall he also reap. For he that soweth to his flesh [lives for *self*] shall of the flesh reap corruption; but he that soweth to the Spirit shall of the Spirit reap life everlasting. And let us not be weary in well doing: for in due season we shall reap, if we faint not" (Gal 6:7-9). We only reap trials and troubles if we have not been faithful. But we reap the power and peace and joy of the Lord if we are faithful, plus a harvest of souls and God's presence to comfort when we do have troubles, as well as eternal reward in glory! Remember, though, there will be no further opportunity to earn rewards after we meet the Lord. It is now or never!

Standing beside the bed of a dying Christian who was weeping, I asked him why he feared death when he knew the Lord was with him. I will always remember his answer: "I'm not weeping because I'm dying. I know I'll be in heaven. The tears come because I've done so little for Christ and wasted so much of my life!"

Why wait until it is too late? "For none of us liveth to himself, and no man dieth to himself. For whether we live, we live unto the Lord; and whether we die, we die unto the Lord: whether we live therefore, or die, we are the Lord's" (Ro 14:7-8).

God's way is easy, so why not take it?

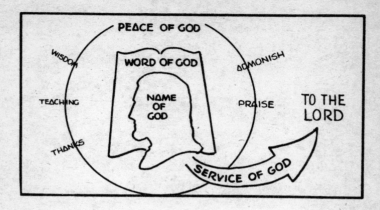

QUESTIONS

1. Who gives peace? (Jn 14:27)
2. What is the answer for worry? (Phil 4:5-7, 9)
3. Why be thankful? (1 Co 15:57; 2 Co 2:14; 9:15; Eph 5:20)
4. What does it mean to allow the Word to dwell in us richly? (Ro 10:8; 1 Th 2:13; 2 Ti 4:2; Titus 1:9; Heb 4:12)
5. Who is to teach the Word? (Phil 1:14; 2:15-16)
6. What are spiritual songs? (Ps 100:2; Eph 5:19-20)
7. What does the name of Christ imply? (Ac 4:12; 10:43; Ro 9:17; 10:13; Eph 1:21; Phil 2:9-10; 2 Ti 2:19)
8. What does lust imply? (Gal 5:16-17; Ja 1:14-15; 1 Pe 2:11)
9. What glorifies God? (Jn 15:14; 2 Th 1:12; 1 Pe 4:11, 14)
10. What are the two kinds of "rewards"? (Mt 16:27; 2 Pe 2:13; Rev 22:12)

14

PLEASING CHRIST

Family, Business, World (Col 3:18—4:6)

IT IS IMPORTANT to "touch base," as it were, before seeing what God commands about the Christian home, and the Christian in the world. Read again Colossians 3:17, 23: "And whatsoever ye do in word or deed, do all in the name of the Lord Jesus, giving thanks to God and the Father by him. And whatsoever ye do, do it heartily, as to the Lord, and not unto men."

This gives the setting and motive for those who are *in Christ* to find God's way easy in everyday relationships.

Testimony in the Family

COLOSSIANS 3:18—"Wives, submit yourselves unto your own husbands, as it is fit in the Lord."

Remember, this is written to the saints *in Christ*, and the Christian home is a threesome: the husband, the wife, and the Lord. "As it is fit in the Lord" has the meaning of being suitable and becoming for a Christian, and it is to fit in with God's will for family relationships as well.

Woman was created to be a help "meet" for man (a companion suitable for him, in contrast to mere animals),

221

but, instead, she stepped out of line and took the lead in disobedience to God. "For Adam was first formed, then Eve. And Adam was not deceived, but the woman being deceived was in the transgression" (1 Ti 2:13-14). Woman has been placed in subjection to her husband.

But Christian wives need not consider subjection as a curse; rather, it is a protection in the Lord. The word *wife* comes from an old English word *weaver,* the one to weave cloth for the family clothing. Single girls were taught to spin thread, and at marriage they were given the mother's loom (the treasure of the family) from which we have the word *heirloom,* while unmarried girls remained as spinners and were called *spinsters.* With marriage came the privilege of inheriting the utensil as well as the right to weave.

Today wives do not weave clothing, but they wash and sew. The delight of the Christian wife should be to "weave her home together in the Lord." What a respon-

THE WEAVER

sibility to know that others are depending upon her, and her home is her mission field to prepare souls for this life as well as for eternity. She has a captive audience!

A woman who loves the Lord will love her husband and children also. Just because a man is growing old and cranky is no reason to neglect him; he needs love all the more! Very often a husband's good nature and love for his wife depend on her attitude of submission and cheerfulness. Cheerfulness! Your home is your kingdom as well as your stage, and you are the queen and the heroine. So be a star! No need to dye your hair to see your husband's eyes light up; just let your own eyes light up when he comes home!

"Who can find a virtuous woman? For her price is far above rubies. The heart of her husband doth safely trust in her. . . . She will do him good and not evil all the days of her life. She seeketh wool, and flax, and worketh willingly with her hands. . . . Strength and honour are her clothing; and she shall rejoice in time to come. She openeth her mouth with wisdom; and in her tongue is the law of kindness. She looketh well to the ways of her household, and eateth not the bread of idleness. Her children arise up, and call her blessed; her husband also, and he praiseth her. . . . Favour is deceitful, and beauty is vain: but a woman that feareth the LORD, she shall be praised" (Pr 31:10-30).

So wives, let your husband and children feel proud that they belong to you. Weave the home together in the Lord!

Maybe you feel that you married a real lemon! Well, no one made you marry him; it was your choice. So just

squeeze that lemon and love him! You are married for better or for worse; so even if you feel you got the "worse," you are still married. God can give grace to bring up your family "in the Lord."

Submitting means that pride must be leveled. Marriages are not made in heaven; they are usually the choice of those involved!

Marriage is not to be entered into lightly, and it is not to be abused, or moved into without the approval of God. "Therefore as the church is subject unto Christ, so let the wives be to their own husbands in everything" (Eph 5:24). The only time this command is superseded is when the husband commands that which is contrary to the Word of God; then the wife is to "obey God rather than man." However, on any matter that does not involve conscience, the wife is to obey her husband even if he is not a Christian (1 Pe 3:1-6).

COLOSSIANS 3:19—"Husbands, love your wives, and be not bitter against them."

Now the shoe is on the other foot! The word *husband* means the "band to hold the house together." The husband is the God-ordained caretaker to lead, to provide for, and to love his family.

The Bible is clear in warning that a Christian is to marry "only in the Lord" (1 Co 7:39). How many heartaches have come from marriage between a Christian and an unbeliever! This unhappiness is part of God's way of showing His disapproval upon the unequal yoke (2 Co 6:14). No one gets away with disobedience to the revealed will of God.

This is also a warning to parents to watch out that children do not "go steady" with unsaved friends, for there is too much likelihood that they will want to get married. Some argue, "But I'm winning him to Christ!" It would be much better to win him to the Lord before becoming his girl at all; we should not do evil that good may come. Marriage will not change character or spiritual condition, and neither will a minister's words in a church ceremony make a marriage "in the Lord" if either member is unsaved. A wedding service has no bearing at all on salvation. If they are not saints *in Christ*, a wedding will not make them so.

A Christian marriage, though, is a beautiful picture of Christ and His bride, the church. "Husbands, love your wives, even as Christ also loved the church, and gave himself for it" (Eph 5:25). As husbands submit themselves to the Lord as their Head, they will take the right attitude toward their wives. This is no slave-and-master relationship, but a partnership and harmony in the Lord, a mutual love-and-respect society!

"As Christ also loved . . . and gave himself" is the Christian spirit in the home. Husband, love your wife! Love, and don't boss! Love, and don't display overbearing aggression and dictatorship!

When these words were inspired, marriages were arranged by brokers. The bride and groom had no selection and did not see each other until the knot was tied! This was also true of old China. In my girlhood I remember attending Christian weddings and seeing the bride heavily veiled in red silk led into the church and seated at the front, and the groom sitting beside her with a small table between them. After the ceremony, he lifted her veil and saw her for the first time! It was a moment of suspense!

Yet, God told Christian husbands to love their wives. There is no choice here! The groom might find himself

THE GROOM HAD NEVER SEEN THE BRIDE !

with an ugly bride or even an ugly-tempered one, but he was to love her! So husband, if your wife is a battle-ax, God says, "Love her!" She might be less of a problem if she had a little more love and attention!

If somewhere along the line Christians have lost their sincere Christian love for their spouses, why not make it a matter of prayer and real effort, and see how God can make them fall in love with each other all over again.

Even at the time of this writing a Christian lady told me how she and her husband have found new love after they heard this lesson in one of my classes. She was so happy, and said, "My husband is so considerate and courteous, I hardly know how to act!"

On the other hand, I know a couple who are so jealous of each other that when one goes forward for the Lord, the other intentionally backslides just to get revenge. It is a constant seesaw of misery.

"So ought men to love their wives as their own bodies. . . . For this cause shall a man leave his father and his mother, and shall be joined unto his wife, and they two shall be one flesh . . . let every one of you in particular so love his wife even as himself; and the wife see that she reverence [respect] her husband" (Eph 5:28-33).

Wives are to respect their husbands, and not to rule the roost and to henpeck them! Too often a woman marries a man to make him over, and then she rejects him because he does not meet her pattern.

Also, mothers-in-law, hands off! Cut those apron strings!

COLOSSIANS 3:20—"Children, obey your parents in all things: for this is well pleasing unto the Lord."

Disobedient children reflect upon their parents and are a shame to the home and the church. "Children, obey your parents in the Lord: for this is right" (Eph 6:1). Here again, these words are only for those "in the Lord," because if a parent is not a Christian, then the youngster must still obey God rather than man. But on things that do not involve conscience before God, the child is to obey even the unsaved parent.

To fail to teach children to obey is to disobey God, and this brings disrepute upon His name as well as making the children unpopular with everyone else. Spoiled youngsters make poor employees and poor employers, poor husbands and wives, and poor parents. They are misfits in society.

Today many push aside God's rule not to spare the rod, and substitute "reason with your child"! It would be fine if they were reasonable, but little children and rebellious teenagers are not always reasonable! So, as long as they are eating and sleeping at home, they should obey their parents.

Parents moan that they "can do nothing with them!" The fact of the matter is, they did nothing with them when they were small; they did nothing about discipline, and very little about family love either.

To "give them everything we never had" is no answer. They become bored and selfish tyrants. The world is now reaping the results of a race of disobedient parents who have raised disobedient children who are now disillusioned and frustrated delinquents.

To obey parents is "well pleasing unto the Lord," Christian youth. You'll be happier; your teachers will be happier; and God will be pleased as well!

COLOSSIANS 3:21—"Fathers, provoke not your children to anger, lest they be discouraged."

Again, God gives another side of the matter. To "provoke" means to irritate by overbearing injustice. Here is the danger of discipline without love and understanding. The unapproachable parent who oversuppresses and keeps the child at a distance, is also disobeying God. This is sin.

Teaching love by example will banish ill-temper and unkindness. How grateful my husband and I are for the lovely Christian girls who married our two sons and are mothers of our grandchildren! Thank God for loving mothers!

Parents need to remember children are children. Constant faultfinding and nagging will discourage anyone, even you! Resentment and a feeling of injustice leave youngsters an easy prey for the rebellious offbeat mobs that defy authority.

One father was so stern and demanding that it was as if he had locked his family in strait jackets. When he died, that family let loose like a jack-in-a-box and flew to all extremes. Someone asked, "But what about the promise of God that if one brings up a child in the way he should go he will not depart from it?" Wait a minute. That father did not train his family—he hog-tied them! To train a child has the meaning of "giving them a taste for the things of God" when they are young, and not just forcing them to obey legalistic rigor.

God bless the women who care for other people's youngsters in the church nursery! This is a real service unto the Lord. The ladies do not complain, yet most parents don't know how their offspring behave in the nursery.

Christian parents, are you letting loose young monsters? Better begin training now; it is never too soon to begin.

Child-training should begin years before they are born! Can we expect obedience from children when we are not obedient to God and are quarreling or ice cold in the home?

Testimony in Business

COLOSSIANS 3:22a—"Servants, obey in all things your masters according to the flesh."

Perhaps the shoe has been pinching a little. Now God turns to the business world.

There will always be differences in social status, even though all believers are *in Christ*. Never does Christ or

Paul tell anyone to expect to change his social standing just because he is converted. In fact, Bible instructions are just the opposite. "Let every man abide in the same calling wherein he was called. Art thou called being a servant? Care not for it [don't let that bother you!]: but if thou mayest be free, use it rather [take advantage of it to serve the Lord]. For he that is called in the Lord, being a servant, is the Lord's freeman: likewise also he that is called, being free, is Christ's servant" (1 Co 7:20-22).

In Paul's time, though, servants really were bondslaves who could not call their life their own. This is what it meant when Christ "took upon him the form of a servant" (Phil 2:7).

A bondslave had no rights as a citizen; Christ laid aside His glory in the presence of God.

A bondslave had no redress in injury; Christ opened not His mouth before His murderers.

A bondslave had no property; Christ had no place to lay His head, and was the poorest of men.

A bondslave could be sold; Christ was sold for thirty pieces of silver, the price of a slave.

A bondslave could be tortured and killed; Christ suffered for us, the just for the unjust, to bring us to God.

"Exhort servants to be obedient unto their own masters, and to please them well in all things; not answering again; not purloining [pilfering], but shewing all good fidelity; that they may adorn the doctrine of God our Saviour in all things" (Titus 2:9-10).

An older man who was just converted, told me of his concern because he had cheated his company out of a sum of money in past years. It had not been missed, but his new conscience in Christ made him want to make amends. He wrote a letter to his former employer and returned the money. Result? That employer was converted!

COLOSSIANS 3:22b—"Not with eyeservice, as menpleasers; but in singleness of heart, fearing God."

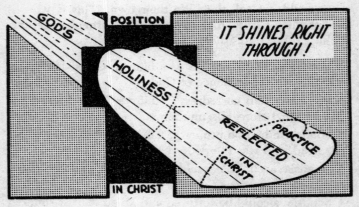

"Menpleasers" are just what it says: those who try to please the boss as long as he is watching, but are lazy, unfaithful and dishonest otherwise. But the Christian is not just serving a human employer; he is serving the Lord. "Singleness of heart" is sincerity instead of two-faced hypocrisy. "Fearing God" does not mean fear of damnation, but rather the fear of displeasing and grieving Him, and the desire to reverence and obey and hold Him in holy awe. God is the real Employer!

COLOSSIANS 4:1—"Masters, give unto your servants that which is just and equal; knowing that ye also have a Master in heaven."

The pattern for employers is courtesy and justice because the Christian employer is also serving the Lord. In the office or the shop, in the army or the medical corps, men can serve the Lord if their testimony is consistent.

Women at home washing dishes can serve the Lord if they love Him and love their family. It is not just public ministry that glorifies the Lord; He sees the motive even more than the ministry. Honesty, integrity, industry and sincerity count for eternity if we love our heavenly Employer!

Testimony in the World

COLOSSIANS 4:5—"Walk in wisdom toward them that are without, redeeming the time."

Those who "are without" are the unsaved without God and without hope, and outside of salvation. The believer is not only to walk like Christ, but to walk for Christ to reach the lost. "He that saith he abideth in him ought himself also so to walk, even as he walked" (1 Jn 2:6), and this walk was a missionary message of love and life. The saint *in Christ* is to be consistent if he is to be insistent! To walk in wisdom will include knowing the Lord, knowing the Word, knowing how to deal with souls, and knowing to get busy *now* before it is too late! "Redeeming the time, because the days are evil" (Eph 5:16).

This means to buy up every opportunity and use every moment in the light of eternity. We will never grow any younger, so it must be now or never.

Time is God's gift, just as salvation is His gift, so it is too precious to squander or waste since it is not our own. To redeem the time costs something of self-sacrifice and real effort, so why are we Christians so lazy and trivial, twittering away our time in foolish nothings and reading fiction and watching soap operas?

The days are evil, for sinful men are becoming worse and worse, and iniquity and lawlessness abound. We see fulfillment of Scripture all around us these days. "Behold, now is the accepted time; . . . now is the day of salvation" (2 Co 6:2) to preach the gospel as well as to accept it. After death it will be too late!

In these last days of the church age, the times of apostasy and departing from the faith, we see a trend toward mere social service which offers only physical benefits to a lost world and neglects the eternal soul. Philanthropy alone is not God's message. A man in a death cell does not want lace curtains at the window; he wants the bars removed! The thirsty man does not want a better house; he craves water! The hungry person does not need a new car; he longs for bread! So God has commissioned the church to preach the gospel. Working for world improvement or civil rights or slum clearance must be secondary to that primary purpose.

God's money should be used to spread the spiritual salvation message or for the benevolence of suffering Christians. All social service should be channeled for this one ultimate purpose: the salvation of souls.

COLOSSIANS 4:6*a*—"Let your speech be alway with grace."

Courtesy and truth untainted—this is grace. God-centered conversation and Scripture-filled doctrine, as well as God-honoring humor, must be balanced with kindness and tact. Grace and truth! Truth alone could sometimes be cold and harsh, but grace softens the facts with love.

COLOSSIANS 4:6*b*—"Seasoned with salt."

What does this mean? Consider the use of salt. First of all, salt makes food appetizing. Have you ever eaten the white of an egg without salt? When there was a shortage of salt in the war days, we learned how insipid our starvation diet could taste! Salt has often been used in the place of money. Salt is a preservative to keep food from rotting. Salt is also a good disinfectant.

Therefore, our speech is to be appetizing and attractive and free from rottenness as we let "no corruption proceed" out of our mouths, and we are to give a soft answer to turn away wrath. This will keep us on our toes!

COLOSSIANS 4:6c—"That ye may know how ye ought to answer every man."

It is still impossible to give answers unless we know the answers, so begin studying and memorizing the Word, and have an answer for others. "Be ready always to give an answer to every man that asketh you a reason of the hope that is in you with meekness and fear: having a good conscience" (1 Pe 3:15-16). Our talk is only as powerful as our walk!

A woman who was recently saved told me how her neighbor had witnessed to her quite effectively until she happened to admit that she seldom went to church. She felt that she could be a good enough Christian without attending church. The convert said, "You know, when she said that, I lost interest in her talking. I saw she was not walking it!"

"Holding fast the faithful word as he hath been taught, that he may be able by sound doctrine both to exhort and to convince the gainsayers" (Titus 1:9).

Paul's desire was that he might speak as he "ought to speak," and this would be in fearlessness, clearness, faithfulness and love. Worship must come before working!

We do not need to know all God's doctrines before we begin to witness, and neither do we have to know all the answers before we give a testimony, but it helps! Begin witnessing as soon as you are saved, but do not stop with those first simple words. Go on to know and to grow!

"Study [make it life's work] to shew thyself approved unto God [by life and lip and learning], a workman that needeth not to be ashamed, rightly dividing the word of truth [rightly handling the Word to understand and give it out]" (2 Ti 2:15).

God's way is the best way!

QUESTIONS

1. Why was woman created? (Gen 2:2-25; 3:20)
2. What does the word *meet* mean? (Ro 1:27; 2 Ti 2:21)
3. What is to be the wife's attitude to her husband? (1 Co 7:34; Titus 2:3-5; 1 Pe 3:1)
4. What does God say about "sparing the rod"? (Pr 13:24; 23:13; 29:15)
5. Should employees obey employers? (Eph 6:5, 9; 1 Ti 6:1-2; 2 Ti 2:21; 1 Pe 2:18)
6. What does God say about "servants"? (Ro 1:1; 6:16; Phil 2:7; 2 Ti 2:24; Titus 1:1; 2:9; 1 Pe 2:16-18; Rev 1:1; 22:3)
7. How to live before the unsaved? (Jn 8:12; Eph 4:1, 17; 1 Th 4:12; 1 Pe 2:12)
8. What does God say about our "time"? (Ro 13:11; 1 Pe 4:2)
9. How can a Christian be savory and attractive for the Lord? (Lk 14:34; 2 Co 2:15; Eph 5:2)
10. Can we know the answer for others? (1 Pe 3:15)

15

PRAYER THROUGH CHRIST
Power in Prayer (Col 4:2-3, 12)

THIS CHAPTER is handled in a different manner than the others, for only the verses on prayer are touched upon, and we will deal with suggestions for power in prayer. Since the verses on prayer are limited, other scriptures are included to bear on this important matter of hints for power in prayer. This is the secret of finding that God's way is easy.

If you have noticed the prayers in the New Testament, you will be impressed that they are definitely for spiritual blessing rather than physical things.

Faith in Prayer

COLOSSIANS 4:2a—"Continue in prayer, and watch in the same."

God would never command us to pray if He could and would not answer. However, prayer is not just telling God a lot of things, but the privilege of fellowship and communion with the Almighty. Rather than praying long prayers, it is much better to be alone with Him for a long time.

To begin with, in order to enter the presence of God,

TALK IT OVER WITH HIM !

we must come by the way He has set forth. "Without faith it is impossible to please him: for he that cometh to God must believe that he is, and that he is a rewarder of them that diligently seek him" (Heb 11:6). The first step, then, in power in prayer is to *seek Him,* and to seek Him as Saviour. The prayer for forgiveness and salvation is the only prayer He will hear from the unsaved heart. When we believe that God is God and can answer prayer, and then ask Him to save us and believe that He will keep His Word, this is faith and we are on praying ground.

This often comes as a shock to those who have been repeatedly saying prayers without knowing God's Word. "The LORD is far from the wicked: but he heareth the prayer of the righteous" (Pr 15:29). The "wicked" is the term referring to those who rejected God in the Old Testament times, and to those who are not *in Christ* in our times. The "righteous" are those *in Christ* and those who received God.

This same principle is repeated in the New Testament. "For the eyes of the Lord are over the righteous, and his ears are open unto their prayers: but the face of the Lord is against them that do evil" (1 Pe 3:12). So, power in prayer begins with contact with God by receiving the Saviour by faith. The prayer which seeks forgiveness and salvation is the only prayer that He will hear from the unsaved heart. But, praise His name, He will hear that!

After a lesson on prayer, a young husband said, "Why, I've been a church member for years and sung in the choir as soloist, and I came to these classes to learn how to teach a Sunday school class! Now I realize that I'm not saved myself! I've never prayed that first prayer to receive Christ."

His wife did not stay to talk that evening, for she felt he was being foolish to want to be saved. She thought she was a Christian because she had been baptized into a church when she was an infant.

It was there in that classroom, though, that her husband prayed his first real prayer, and went home rejoicing in knowing contact with God. When I suggested that he deal with his wife, he was dubious. "I don't know about her," he said. "She was raised in another religion!"

However, when they reached home they found their furnace had broken down, and they spent most of the night trying to repair it. As they worked and waited, they talked. It was in the early hours of that next morning that his wife realized that the many prayers she had said, as prescribed by her church, had never been answered, for she had never received Christ as her personal Saviour.

In the cold house she gave her heart to the Lord as they prayed together.

Now in a Bible-believing church, they are serving the Lord in youth work and Sunday school, as well as singing for the glory of God. A more faithful couple one could not find. But it had to begin with the prayer of faith seeking *Him*.

Once a person becomes a saint *in Christ*, the prayer of faith is to believe God's promises and power to hear. The One who invites us to continue in prayer and watch for answers is the Almighty who controls the whole universe as well as being interested in our personal lives. And the prayer of faith implies that we believe He knows best and is working all things together for good to them that love Him. Faith in prayer does not try to run God, but rather lets Him run us! If He knows how many hairs we have on our heads, can He not unscramble our daily problems?

There is no surprise or accident as far as His loved ones

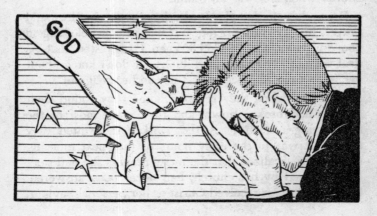

are concerned, for everything is for good (whether we might like it or not!) and even the laws of nature are but the thoughts of the God who said, "Cast thy burden upon the Lord, and he shall sustain thee" (Ps 55:22). He has not promised to remove trials, but to sustain us. He does no unnecessary miracles! So take your burdens to the Lord and leave them there; do not drag them off again to the neighbors or friends; leave them there!

Faith in prayer is to let God solve the problems and not to dictate to Him. He knows our needs, but He tells us to come and to bring them to Him. And when we pray, He gives us more than we need! He is "able to do exceeding abundantly above all that we ask or think" (Eph 3:20). He has not promised to abdicate His throne and let us tell Him what to do, but He has invited us to "come boldly unto the throne of grace, that we may obtain mercy, and find grace to help in time of need" (Heb 4:16). He also tells us, "Behold, I am the Lord, the God of all flesh: is there any thing too hard for me?" (Jer 32:27). There can be no freedom from anxiety when we leave Him out of our plans.

Colossians 4:2—"Continue in prayer, and watch in the same with thanksgiving."

The prayer of faith will watch for answers. However, be sure that you are not claiming what God has not promised. It is not faith to be foolish! His answer may be to give us patience to wait for His time, or it may be to make us willing not to want what we think we must have, or it may be to supply the need in some other way than we expected, or it may be to give us something better for us, or it may be even to make us realize that what we asked was not according to His will and for His glory. Faith is to believe God will do what is best, and He will make His way easy.

Watch in thanksgiving! Prayer and praise go together, for praise offered even before we see the answers is proof that we trust Him. Trials constrain us to spend more time with Him, and sometimes they are the only thing that will bring us to our knees. Prayer is the fulcrum on which to place our heartaches. When Christians moan, "I'm so blue and depressed, and I don't know why!" God says, "I don't know why either, for I'm still on the throne!"

Prayer has a twofold work. Subjectively, it makes us willing for God's will; objectively, in some marvelous way He has promised to answer our petitions when we come according to His will. "Call upon me in the day of trouble: I will deliver thee, and thou shalt glorify me" (Ps 50:15). But notice how this promise is qualified: "Offer unto God thanksgiving; and pay thy vows unto the most High. Whoso offereth praise glorifieth me" (Ps 50:14, 23).

Faithfulness in Prayer

COLOSSIANS 4:3—"Withal praying also for us, that God would open unto us a door of utterance, to speak the mystery of Christ, for which I am also in bonds."

What a faithful Christian Paul was! Faithful even unto death! Power in prayer depends upon our personal faithfulness to the Lord. Paul's request was that he might be fearless even though it might cost him further martyrdom. He was indeed fearless and was finally beheaded as a martyr in Rome.

Not only does power in prayer depend upon faith in God, but it produces faithfulness in His saints. Power in prayer is not hindered because of Him, but because we are unfaithful to Him. He promises, "If ye abide in me, and my words abide in you, ye shall ask what ye will, and it shall be done unto you" (Jn 15:7). To "abide" is to be faithful and obedient, which is a master key that opens the treasure-house of power in prayer. To live right is to pray right. "Go and bring forth fruit . . . that whatsoever ye shall ask of the Father in my name, he may give it you" (Jn 15:16).

Here is clear qualification for power in prayer: "Whatsoever we ask, we receive of him, because we keep his commandments, and do those things that are pleasing in his sight" (1 Jn 3:22). It is better to comply with His will than to complain! The only way to command God is to obey Him. So much depends upon our willingness for His will and our own condition of fellowship with Him. Paul was not asking to be free from bonds, or an open door from his prison, but an open door to preach the gospel. What a contrast this is to so many prayers which are little more than a recital of selfish wants!

Listen to God's heart cry: "O that there were such an heart in them, that they would fear me, and keep all my commandments always, that it might be well with them, and with their children for ever" (Deu 5:29).

COLOSSIANS 4:4—"That I may make it manifest, as I ought to speak."

What an unselfish request! Even as for Israel, so God's desire for us is that we be faithful to Him. "What doth the LORD thy God require of thee, but to *fear* the LORD thy God, to *walk* in all his ways, and to *love* him, and to *serve* the LORD thy God with all thy heart and with all thy soul, to *keep* the commandments of the LORD, and his statutes, which I command thee this day for thy good?" (Deu 10:12-13). Did you hear that? "For thy good?" This is the reason we do well when we obey and love and are faithful. It is for our good as well as to see power in prayer!

Fervency in Prayer

COLOSSIANS 4:12a—"Epaphras, who is one of you, a servant of Christ, saluteth you, always labouring fervently for you in prayers."

What an example Epaphras was! As a servant of Christ he was also a servant of the saints (Col 1:7) and a man of fervency in prayer. Genuine prayer is the soul's sincere desire and heart-to-heart contact with the Lord of heaven and earth. When prayer counts little with us, then it counts little with God too!

"The effectual fervent prayer of a righteous man availeth much" (Ja 5:16*b*). Thus prayer must come from a righteous man who has been saved by faith *in Christ* and is also in fellowship with Him. It is effectual because it is offered by the saint who is led by the Spirit of God (Ro 8:26-27) and is willing for His will. It is fervent because it is sincere and earnest instead of flippant and shallow. "Delight thyself also in the LORD; and he shall give thee the desires of thine heart. Commit thy way unto the LORD; trust also in him; and he shall bring it to pass" (Ps 37:4-5). Bring what to pass? Our way? No! When we give up our way to the Lord, He takes it and makes it His way, so He brings His way to pass.

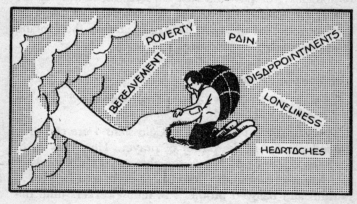

Fervency is not some whipped-up frenzy of emotional effort. Requests bring answers that come from the earnest heart of a saint *in Christ* who is willing for God's will.

Fervency links our efforts with the energy of God. Real and fervent prayer is labor, and labor costs; it costs time, strength, self-denial, persistence and, most of all, holiness. Are we willing to pay the price?

Often so-called prayers are merely the empty repetition of platitudes that we really do not desire. We pray for the missionaries but do not give toward their work; we pray for our church but do not attend faithfully; we pray for souls but do not witness; we know we should ask for the right things, but they are not our real desires. We cannot fool God! So why do we try?

Delays are not necessarily denials, for He has not promised *when* He will answer or *what* He will answer or *how* He will answer. To stop praying because we are too lazy, or too busy, or have no real earnestness, makes us the "have not" Christians because we "ask not." It might be well to pray that the Lord change us, rather than asking Him to change everyone else!

Fittingness in Prayer

COLOSSIANS 4:12b—"That ye may stand perfect and complete in all the will of God."

The Christians mentioned in Colossians 4 are certainly a good witness to the power of prayer. How they fit in with the will of God! Notice the phrases "faithful minister and fellowservant in the Lord . . . comfort your hearts . . . faithful and beloved brother . . . fellowworkers unto the kingdom of God, which have been a comfort . . . a great zeal . . . beloved physician . . . the ministry which thou hast received in the Lord."

Could such things be said of you and me? Are we fitting in with the will of God?

Prayers are sometimes offered up, but nothing comes down! Could it be that our requests do not fit in with Him? All the promises regarding prayer are qualified. For example, "This is the confidence that we have in him, that, if we ask any thing according to his will, he heareth us" (1 Jn 5:14). God wants to mold the one who prays into His own mind, and then the prayer will be according to His will.

Sometimes prayer is used as a sort of fetish to ward off evil or to bring good, or we ask too ardently for the wrong things and too languidly for the right. So foolish we are!

Neither is prayer a religious emergency measure for those who are not in fellowship with the Lord, nor a "spare tire" when all else fails!

Too often the core of *self* is right in the center of prayer requests. It is only when the outer coating of pious word-

ing is melted away by the all-seeing eye of God that the camouflage is peeled away. Then the Spirit of God can deal with that hard core of self, and prayer can be answered.

He loves us too much to give us all we ask for in our ignorance. "The Spirit also helpeth our infirmities: for we know not what we should pray for as we ought: but the Spirit itself [Himself] maketh intercession for us" (Ro 8:26). Since we really do not know what to ask, let us stop trying to tell Him what to do and, rather, let Him direct our paths. Begin each day with Bible study and prayer, for this shows what value we place upon communion with our Lord, and through this means He can touch us.

A little boy was crying to play with a shiny new butcher knife on the kitchen table. His mother moved it away from him, and he cried harder and stamped his little feet. She was about to administer discipline when she thought,

I'll just let him have the knife! She handed it to him. His tear-stained face lit up with glee. But it was short-lived. A few minutes later he was crying again. Nothing serious, but a few drops of blood on the floor from his cut finger cured him of ever asking for the knife again!

Remember how the children of Israel demanded much from God in their rebelliousness, and "he gave them their request; but sent leanness into their soul" (Ps. 106:15)? They wished they did not have what they had requested!

God does no unnecessary miracles. Never forget this! He has not promised to heal every sickness, even for Christians, and He has not promised long life on this earth. But He does promise grace (2 Co 12:9).

"For we know that the whole creation [animals and men] groaneth and travaileth in pain together until now [ever since God cursed the earth because of sin]. And not only they, but ourselves also, which have the first-fruits of the Spirit, even we ourselves groan within ourselves, waiting for the adoption, to wit [which is], the redemption of our body" (Ro 8:22-23). At the resurrection we shall have a perfect body. In the meantime we are still under the physical curse of sin.

Watch out for the danger of claiming promises God has not given for our church age. Be careful not to pick up the Bible, open it at random and apply every verse, regardless of its context and dispensation. This is where errors spring up.

God will not do unnecessary miracles. He has not promised to drop food from heaven when we have the sense and ability to earn our living. He has not promised to supply luxuries or to keep money coming in when we spend foolishly or for sinful things. He has not promised a big bank account or a big family or big success here on earth. But He has promised spiritual health (if we desire it), eternal life in glory, souls for our hire, and treasure laid up in heaven, plus the extra bonus of victory over sin (if we desire it) and grace for suffering.

Time in prayer makes the saint *in Christ* a sharp tool for the Lord's service. It is possible to work without praying, but praying will make work fruitful; you cannot pray without working!

A passing traveler saw a mountain man sawing a pile of wood with a very dull saw, so he stopped to ask, "Why don't you sharpen your tool?"

The fellow wiped his brow, stretched, and drawled, "Waal, effen I do, I'd haffer saw too much more wood!"

Are we trying to live for God without prayer, and finding we are working with a dull tool? Jesus promised, "And whatsoever ye shall ask in my name, that will I do, that the Father may be glorified in the Son. If ye shall ask any thing in my name, I will do it. If ye love me, keep my commandments" (Jn 14:13-15).

The promises of God are like a checkbook full of spiritual riches. This is quite different from our own checkbook, where we tear out a check but cannot use it again. Instead, the checks in God's book can be used over and over again!

For example: "But my God shall supply all your need according to his riches in glory by Christ Jesus" (Phil 4:19).

"My God" is the Owner of all the wealth of heaven and

earth as well as the One who loved me and gave Himself for me. He is our *Banker!*

"In glory" is the *address* of the *bank* where thieves cannot break through and steal!

"According to his riches" shows the deposit available. Limitless riches!

"Shall supply" is the promise to pay on demand to all who come according to His will.

"All your need" is but a drop in the bucket in comparison to the supply available.

"By Christ Jesus" is the signature that brings power in prayer. God's promise checkbook is only for those who are *in Christ*, and for those things which He would endorse.

The question is, Just what is our need? This is where many make a mistake. Perhaps we need patience, kindness and grace in a trial, but we ask for freedom from the trial. Perhaps we need humility and economy, but we ask for success and material things. Too often we think we need money, health and prosperity, and we shrink from deprivation and pain. God will supply the need, and He knows what we need. Are we really willing for His will?

You have seen the will of God as given in the book of Colossians, but have you received Him? Are you *in Christ*? If not, will you do so even now as you lay down this book? God grant it! Find out that God's way is easy when we let Him take control, and God's way is easy when we are willing for Him to lead the way.

"But the wisdom that is from above is first pure, then peaceable, gentle, and *easy* to be intreated, full of mercy and good fruits, without partiality, and without hypocrisy. And the fruit of righteousness is sown in peace of them that make peace" (Ja 3:17-18).

God's way is indeed easy!

WITH A MANSION PROVIDED —
why live in a shack?

PRAYER PRIVILEGE

PRAYER PRACTISE

Call unto me, and I will answer thee, and show thee great and mighty things, which thou knowest not. Jer. 33:3.

QUESTIONS

1. To whom should we pray? (Mt 6:9; Ac 12:5)
2. Through whom should we pray? (Jn 14:13-14)
3. With whose help do we pray? (Ro 8:26-27)
4. What is the prayer of repentance? (Ps 19:12; Lk 18:10-14; Ac 8:22; 1 Jn 1:9)
5. Why keep on praying? (Lk 18:1; Ro 12:12; 1 Th 5:17)
6. What do we do about our burdens? (Phil 4:6)
7. What are some of the hindrances to prayer? (Ps 66:18; Pr 1:24-28; 28:9; Is 59:1-2; Ja 4:3; 1 Pe 3:7)
8. What is fervent prayer? (Mt 21:22; Ac 12:5; Ja 1:5-8)
9. What is the will of God in prayer? (Ps 37:4-5; Jn 14:13-14)
10. For what should we pray? (Ps 106:4-5; Ro 1:9; Eph 6:8, 19-20; 2 Th 3:1-2)

KAY FRIEDERICHSEN BOOKS

GOD'S WAY MADE EASY, GOD'S RELIEF FOR BURDENS, GOD'S WORD MADE PLAIN, GOD'S WILL MADE CLEAR, PROPHECY UNVEILED — REVELATION SIMPLIFIED, LIKE THEM THAT DREAM (testimony of God's goodness during the war years in the Philippines).